PANOPTICON

THE
SEAGULL
LIBRARY OF
GERMAN
LITERATURE

HANS MAGNUS ENZENSBERGER

PANOPTICON

TWENTY TEN-MINUTE ESSAYS

Translated by Tess Lewis

LONDON NEW YORK CALCUTTA

GOETHE INSTITUT

This publication has been supported by a grant
from the Goethe-Institut India

Seagull Books, 2022

First published as
Enzensbergers Panoptikum. Zwanzig Zehn-Minuten-Essays
© Suhrkamp Verlag Berlin, 2012

First published in English translation by Seagull Books, 2018
English translation © Tess Lewis, 2018

Published as part of the Seagull Library of German Literature, 2022

ISBN   978 1 8030 9 043 6

British Library Cataloguing-in-Publication Data
A catalogue record for this book is available from the British Library

Typeset by Seagull Books, Calcutta, India
Printed and bound by WordsWorth India, New Delhi, India

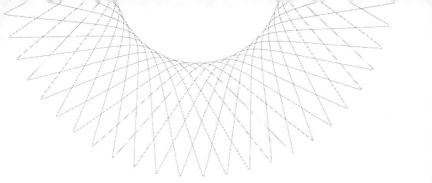

CONTENTS

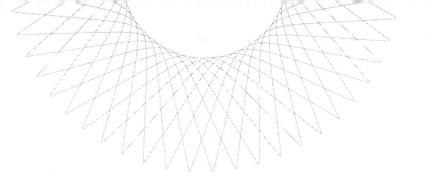

INSTEAD OF A BLURB

Is this serious? Can someone who is not a philosopher distinguish problems that have a solution from those that have none? Can he explain how nations are created at desks without writing a standard work in the field? Yes, it is possible. Short texts on enormous subjects are nothing new, they have been around for five hundred years. The great forefather of the essay, Michel de Montaigne, showed us how it's done: he wrote *On Sadness*, *On the Disadvantage of High Rank*, *On Cannibals* and did so following his mood and inspiration yet without exhausting either the reader or the topic.

But what, exactly, is meant by 'enormous subjects'? Nothing was too trivial for Montaigne; he knew how to shine a new light on thumbs, on sleep, even on diversions. And a few hundred lines were usually enough. 'He never wrote a book when a page would do, and never a chapter when a word was enough.' This was Lichtenberg's method as well.

I freely admit that thoroughness is not my strong suit. Where did this first person suddenly come from, this pronoun not usually found in blurbs or in jacket copy? It has to do with the imaginary place the observer occupies when he is a part of what he notices, what he finds astonishing, and what he tries to describe. Therefore, 'I' must also take the blame. And because there is always someone who knows better and more than I do, I gladly quote my auxiliaries and informants, just like my incomparable forefather. The old man could dispense with footnotes and commentary because his readers were as familiar with the classics as he was. They didn't rely on the Internet the way we do.

Who knows what a panopticon is these days? If you type the word in a search bar, you're immediately sent off on a wrong tack to an Englishman named Jeremy Bentham. He was a formidable jurist who designed an ideal prison in his free time. A single watchman was to sit in the dark and oversee as many prisoners as possible. Such institutions were, in fact, constructed. Soon enough shrewd entrepreneurs realized that this dubious invention could reduce the cost of production and increase the efficiency in factories.

I have nothing of the sort in mind, although I would like to maintain a panoptic view insofar as is possible. I'd rather remind my readers of another meaning of the word: Karl Valentin called the cabinet of curiosities and horrors he opened in the mid-1930s his *Panoptikum*. In it viewers could admire, along with implements of torture, all manner of abnormalities and sensational inventions.

Step right up, ladies and gentlemen! You won't regret it.

MICROECONOMICS

What economists mean by economics is, at best, clear to them; the rest of the world has certain doubts about the concept and wonder if this branch of the social sciences has anything scientific about it at all. Economists have institutes, endowed chairs and a secure income at their disposal, and their economic activity has little to do with that of housewives, pensioners or children. Economists prefer to concern themselves with large aggregates and masses of statistical data. Most of them weave together odd strands of theories that, for some reason, are always considered neoclassical. Listening to them, you would think we live in an idyllic, fairy-tale world. You'd be astonished to hear that, despite fluctuations, the market inevitably tends towards a state of equilibrium. It is efficient, it corrects and optimizes itself, and all those who are part of it behave perfectly rationally. These assumptions are accepted as givens even though they are simply hypotheses that are unverified, if not unverifiable.

Following the provisional demise of Communism, neoclassical theory offered itself as a replacement for the lost utopia. Although of rather meagre constitution, it wasn't stingy with promises and did not lack adherents. Towards the end of the twentieth century, it had been undernourished with complex mathematical models of risk management. Economists never shied away from making claims about the future, and the fact that they regularly made fools of themselves with their predictions never led them to question their overall competence.

This does not mean, however, that their guild is free from bitter infighting and factionalism as is part and parcel of other disciplines. For decades Keynesians and monetarists have battled for supreme authority. Technical analysts would not, at any price, want to be confused with fundamental analysts or market-trend researchers. Recently there have even been economists who ascribe to the view that in classical theory most people exist only as abstract quantities. They are reduced, according to this logic, to their respective roles. They are either wage earners, consumers, investors, shareholders, entrepreneurs or depositors, and in each of these roles they are guided by a single interest: to maximize their economic advantage and nothing else.

Some classical authors were already much more advanced. The idea that economic decisions were based on *rational choice* was completely foreign to them. In *Fable of the Bees*, Bernard Mandeville claimed that private vices—like falsehood, extravagance and pride—were what made public prosperity possible. And Adam Smith followed suit, somewhat less polemically, with his famous image of the 'invisible hand' that turns the

2

irrational choices made by individuals to serve the general good.

The dominant neoclassical school of thought had no interest in all this. And yet, this school of thought has lately come under pressure from a new tendency. Behavioural economists spotted a yawning gap. They want to understand why people don't behave the way most economists expect them to. Behavioural economists have abandoned the tenet of the rational *homo economicus*, but not the ambition to develop the neatest possible models. In pursuit of this aim, they rely on the one hand on empirical procedures, tests and surveys, and on the other on mathematical models like game theory or on theorems of evolutionary biology or social psychology.

Whether or not they've managed in this way to see into the puzzling behaviour of 'economic subjects' is open to debate. Their ambition to emulate the hard sciences leads them to reduce human beings in their calculations to statistical phantoms. These unfortunate researchers' love of abstraction is constantly getting in their way. They apparently are as little able to change their own spots as those of the people they are studying.

And yet, the latter are known to be susceptible to all possible moods, illusions, fads and habits. They are as disposed to panic as to inertia, wilfulness and the herd instinct. Many are ready to sacrifice anything at all in order to save face, to indulge in their erotic predilections, or to maintain *la bella figura*. Economists must find this behaviour regrettable, unreasonable and ignorant. To be sure, quantifying addiction and fear, confidence and rashness, irascibility and defiance is a Sisyphean task. Those questioned undermine the interviews, surveys and tests because they not only lie unrestrainedly to those asking the questions but also to themselves. Furthermore, they routinely defy the simplest economic rules.

Most of their daily transactions take place outside the flow of money and credit. They raise children without demanding adequate compensation. They enter into relationships without insuring themselves against possible loan defaults or even drawing up a reasonable profit and loss statement. Sometimes they work for free, let golden opportunities pass out of sheer orneriness, throw their money out the window, waste valuable time, follow their horoscopes or some religious fatwa, give away all sorts of things without expecting anything in return, and carry on in this vein to the theoreticians' despair.

A vast dark expanse opens up around our species' actual economic practices. The generally accepted concepts of black market, grey market and dirty money fall short and are inadequate to describe the informal economy. To shine a little light on the subject one must examine the details, for better or worse, and that requires forgoing generalizations and leaving the economy to the economists, even if the professionals aren't allowed to do so. Such a microeconomy could function with little outlay and begin with research into the circles of their families and acquaintances. Half a dozen subjects would easily be enough to demonstrate that a marvellous diversity reigns in this area.

Look, for example, at the Polish aunt who takes a twelve-hour bus ride every two weeks to care for her semi-paralysed mother and then returns to Germany on the same route to clean houses. She has never filled out an official form, has no bank account, pays no taxes and accepts only cash. She is, nevertheless, fiercely honest since she knows that Jesus would not approve of anything less.

Similarly, the entrepreneur bursting with ideas and constantly starting new companies defies any attempt at categorization. As soon as he begins making a profit, he leaves the flourishing enterprise because the routine of success bores him to death and because, he claims, 'he doesn't need money.'

Nor should we overlook the noble spirit and bibliophile who gladly invites his acquaintances to first-class restaurants, but realizes with a grimace of pain as soon as the waiter brings the bill that he has forgotten his wallet.

There is also the family doctor with a passion for singing, who enrols in a music academy but misses a string of rehearsals because once a year he travels to Burundi or the Congo for weeks at a time, not only offering medical services to Doctors Without Borders but also to child soldiers and warlords. We can assume that he pays for his plane tickets out of his own pocket.

No one understands why the gardener who comes to the house three times a year forgets to send a bill despite repeated reminders and even though the bank has cut his credit. His only explanation is that he has other, more urgent worries. And how can it be that the renowned novelist can't find a publisher for his new book; that he has no money, yet pays his cook and his secretary punctually; that the corner store no longer gives him credit so he makes do with a fried egg and a roll for dinner.

Economists, as every newspaper reader knows, never cease to be astonished and irritated by the utterly irrational behaviour of the so-called (and erroneously labelled) average consumer yet they themselves are not exempt from it. In fact, among financiers and their advisors this irrationality reaches the highest degree. One Nobel Prize winning–economist precipitates a bankruptcy that makes Wall Street tremble. Barely released from prison, the investment banker whose Ponzi schemes earned him three years in the nick heads straight to Singapore or Dubai to start up a new hedge fund. And the solitary day trader in New York is sleep deprived because the Tokyo Stock Exchange opens at three in the morning, so he has to have a bag of cocaine at hand in the bathroom day and night to stay awake.

Such phenomena appear most often in the newspapers' business sections when enormous amounts of money are involved. There is little public discussion of the others. They no doubt travel in circles far removed from any textbooks in economic zones about which academia can offer no information. Only now and then will a TV programme offer a fleeting glimpse into these obscure areas, like the reality TV show *Raus aus den Schulden* [Get Yourself Out of Debt]. That such insights might be turned into coherent generalizations is almost too much to hope for, or to fear. In short, anyone who would like to know what people do and what drives them should perhaps look in the mirror. He would realize soon enough that his economic rationality is no more advanced than that of those people whose economic irrationality never ceases to amaze him.

ON INSOLUBLE PROBLEMS

Because my knowledge of Greek is not particularly extensive, I've had to consult the dictionary. It seems as if *problem* did not originally signify a question proposed for a solution or a set task but something thrown at one's feet, as the word is comes from the verb *ballein*, to throw. *Pro-blem*, thrown forward.

Still, that's only half of the truth. For every person who tries, as much as possible, to wait problems out, to suppress or delay them, there are at least a dozen who long for them and, in fact, crave them all the more the harder they are. The more entangled they become, the more stubbornly they search for a solution. The addictiveness of this craving is often underestimated, whether in a computer game or in an issue of geopolitical dimensions.

Many people get their regular dose in the daily crossword puzzle. Those who aim higher can rack their brains over Fermat's Last Theorem. That's what happened with the British mathematician Andrew Wiles. He stumbled on this well-known but never-proven theorem. Twenty-three years later, after a few serious setbacks, he was able to present his definitive proof of the theorem and became world famous. Countless others who tried throughout the centuries to square the circle were less fortunate. The solution to this problem is that it has no solution. This conclusion we owe to a certain Mr von Lindemann from Freiburg who published his proof in 1882. This, too, was a triumph. He spared future amateurs the trouble of struggling against this insurmountable obstacle like wasps against a living-room window.

Accordingly, it is helpful to distinguish between problems that have a solution and those that have none. Unfortunately, this is easier said than done. Even mathematicians have difficulties separating the two categories neatly despite the heroic efforts of writers like Gödel and Turing to bring a little clarity to their contemporaries and to posterity, at least on this topic.

There are, namely, apparently simple tasks that can be solved in principle but the amount of time and calculation capacity needed is so astronomically high that it is better to leave them unsolved. A sales representative who must meet with a certain number of clients might face such a problem. He will mark their locations on his map and then will figure out the shortest route required to see each and every client. He will pull out his hair when he realizes that the number of possible routes increases out of all proportion as the number of clients grows. With 20 clients, he would have several billion possibilities to choose from. If he wanted to try them all, he would not only have to give up his career but also live longer than the planet. There is no practical solution for the travelling salesman. He would have to settle for approximate solutions. For this, mathematicians have come up with a number of tricks that have become ever-more refined over time. They come ever nearer to their goal, but will never ever reach it *completely*.

Physicians wrestle with the same difficulties, beginning with turbulence in the bathtub. No system of equations can describe it exactly. A few raindrops on a sea as smooth as glass can let loose a muddle of waves, the dynamics of which we cannot calculate. (In any case, in the world of subatomic particles, normal human reason does not apply.)

Claims about the future are even less reassuring. No one, so far, has been able to predict the next earthquake or volcanic eruption. And as everyone who has tried to plan a holiday knows, even the best weather forecasts for the coming week can quickly go south. Natural scientists know this because they're familiar with the bugs in complex systems. A single grain of sand can bring down the side of a high dune. Exactly when and whether a critical condition is reached can often be determined only once it's too late. Behind most problems that science has solved lurk a host of new questions without evident answers. The number of problems to be solved will, therefore, never decrease but only increase. Researchers never need to fear not having enough work. And if things are so uncertain in the hard sciences, how much more confused must be our capacity to explain the world around us? There are, to be sure, signs of progress wherever one looks. Processes of industrial production can be optimized up to a certain level. Logistics experts minimize friction. Safety tests minimize risks. International norms make devices compatible, when we're lucky.

But as soon as you have to deal with people rather than machines, rationalization reaches its limit and chaos reigns. Neither the fastest computer programs, nor the most elaborate statistical methods, nor even the most beautiful models of probability calculation can change this. Most fiascos occur precisely in those areas where the most time and money is spent. Financial markets are particularly susceptible. In a single edition of an economic journal one can find advice, recommendations and warnings that completely contradict one another. Most fund managers perform no better than a random stock market index. Word has it that there are elderly ladies whose investment decisions over tea surpass those of any investment advisor. The average success rate of experts is close to that of a random number generator. One can only shake one's head in wonder at the self-confidence of so-called analysts who proclaim a new fallacy every single day without ever doubting their infallibility.

Politicians, usually paid much less than the augurs of capital, have a comparable success rate. Still, one feels much more sorry for them. They, too, are forced to make decisions knowing the consequences are unforeseeable. The independent variables are far too numerous, the secondary effects and reactions unclear. However, they,

unlike the traders, are held accountable for what they cause.

Their voters never dream of distinguishing between solvable and insolvable problems. Politicians must always give the impression of being on top of everything. 'I have no idea'; 'We'll see how it turns out'; 'Take a deep breath and jump'—the more appropriate these answers are, the less politicians can afford to give them. And so, those responsible fall back ever-more frequently on the claim, 'There is no alternative', which is meant to banish all doubts, even in the face of aporia they are powerless to resolve. To admit as much, however, would simply weaken their hand.

That is why a government cannot afford to distinguish between solvable and insolvable problems. Unfortunately, the more closely one looks, the more one sees that the latter predominate. There is no lack of examples to illustrate this. Every minister of health can tell you a thing or two. Not only does he have to deal with the population's countless complaints rather than its well-being—which is why the title is a misnomer—but he is also not to be envied because the system for which he is responsible is hopeless, overstretched. All attempts to reform the system have foundered on a barbed-wire tangle of conflicting interests. Hospitals, doctors, nurses, health insurance providers and pharmaceutical companies are all guided by competing interests. On top of it all, the unfortunate minister must also keep in mind millions of patients, a not-inconsiderable block of voters.

Rapidly rising costs explode every conceivable budget, and it is easy to imagine that demographic growth will unhinge the entire system sooner or later. All that is left for the minister to do is muddle through, to try and buy time, to find a compromise that will strengthen the existing system rather than attempt to resolve the system's contradictions.

The minister of health is in good company: a politician in the department of education who aspires to offering all students equal opportunity and to sort out the mess in his field; a minister of finance who intends to clear the absurd thicket of the tax code; a chancellor who wants to keep the financial markets on a tight leash. Each of them faces opponents he will never defeat.

Mathematicians are lucky. They can invoke logical reasons why certain problems have no solution. This rationality is foreign to human societies. The most perfect, most carefully vetted plan, approved by every possible official begins to totter if a critical mass of voters calls it into question. Confidence suddenly collapses and there's a run on the banks. If there's a report of a nuclear disaster, iodine tablets run out. One idiotic interview, the mood shifts and the election is lost. It's always people who disrupt business. Their obstreperousness undermines every calculation.

Only one conclusion is possible. Politics is the art of the impossible. Those who prefer clear, straightforward, obvious solutions should find another profession.

The most demanding might be tempted by number theory; those who are satisfied with less might consider passing the time with a game of solitaire in the hope that they can complete it and enjoy a measure of success that is as beautiful as it is fleeting.

HOW TO INVENT NATIONS AT YOUR DESK

The Germanic peoples naturally did not know they were Germanic. It was the Greeks and Romans who taught them this. More precisely, it was a handful of writers whose works they never read: Plutarch, Julius Caesar and, especially, Publius Cornelius Tacitus' famous work *Germania* from 98 CE, a full twenty-five pages, with which the Germans refreshed their spirit many centuries later. I remember an old school atlas. I was in seventh grade, poring over a map of the so-called Migration Period. Colourful arrows showed which bands of peoples were wandering around Central Europe at the time. Impossible to name them all: the Quadi and the Rugii, the Veleti and the Chauci, the Heruli and the Chatti, and of course the Cherusci. The more I delved into this tangled picture, the more uneasy I felt, and I began to doubt that these tribes ever existed.

The Bible also gave me something to chew over. Would we ever have heard of the Canaanites, the Tribe of Asher, the Levites, or the Maccabees if that bestseller had not mentioned them? At any rate, these were not nations but obscure tribes, ethnic groups, sects or merely family clans.

The situation is similar elsewhere, for example, in the Caucasus. If you want to find your bearings there, you'd be well advised to find yourself a Caucasologist. He will explain that dozens of ethnic groups live together in a small territory. Not only do their religions and customs differ sharply—giving rise to endless conflicts—but they also speak 40 to 70 fundamentally different languages, along with hundreds of dialects, in various alphabets.

It is no surprise that anyone who understands this will hesitate if asked, when entering the United States, if he is Caucasian. This does not mean, however, that anyone suspects him of being Chechen or Ingush. The word *Caucasian* is simply a euphemism for a white-skinned person, at least as long as he does not come from Latin America. In that case, he would be categorized as Latino even if he doesn't speak a word of Latin.

If the question concerns one's mother tongue rather than one's ancestry, then Anglophones and most South Americans, as well as the French and Germans, belong to a much larger group. They are all Indo-European, also known in Germany as *Indogermanen*. Unfortunately, it would be difficult to find these people outside the field of linguistics. And there is no evidence of the language named after them. Their vocabulary consists of syllables that were 'deduced' if not quite simply invented and therefore are marked with a small asterisk in dictionaries.

But how is it then with nations to which we belong, whether we like it or not, merely because we were not born just anywhere but in the place where someone registered the fact of our birth. Natio means, quite simply, 'birth' and only secondly 'a group of individuals united by a factor forming a people, tribe, clan, class or throng.' As to the question of when nations of the kind that regularly gather in New York were first formed, well, historians and experts of international law have filled entire libraries. Suffice it to say that my contribution will be modest, a mere footnote that will nonetheless attempt an answer.

It seems to me as if most nations that attend the General Assembly on the East River were invented by a handful of retiring scholars within the last two hundred years. There were, indeed, a few scattered precursors whose ideas influenced these authors but only in 1800 was a critical mass reached. It began like this: several researchers sat at their desks examining what the so-called vernacular had to say. They collected folk tales, idiomatic expressions, riddles, songs and legends with admirable zeal. It was a pleasant and innocent pastime.

Most of these gentlemen wore stiff collars and spoke German. They hailed from places like Mohrungen, Hanau and Ehrenbreitstein. Some made their living as tutors or pastors, others had not only achieved a certain renown but even held university chairs. One of the earliest members of this flock of writers bore the title Superintendent General, which sounds much worse than it was since the bearer, Johann Gottfried Herder, still had adequate time to devote himself to his studies in tranquil Weimar. He gave the German language a hand, coining new words like *Zeitgeist* [spirit of the age] or *Weltmarkt* [global market]. Even the *Volkslied* [folk song] didn't exist before he invented it—or, at least, there had been no word for it. He was one of the earliest collectors of this music. Herder didn't restrict himself to his native traditions, but cast a wide net. Polyglot that he was, he also translated folk songs from Spanish, Old Norse, Lithuanian and half a dozen other languages. It may sound strange to our ears but his work set off an avalanche.

When Achim von Armin and Clemens Brentano arrived on the scene a few years later with their collection of German folk songs and poems, *Des Knaben Wunderhorn* [The Boy's Magic Horn: Old German Songs], the brakes were off. Jacob and Wilhelm Grimm edited a collection of ancient German, Icelandic and Scottish stories and their book of fairy tales became a worldwide bestseller. Suddenly hoary manuscripts were being deciphered and sagas, sayings and ballads flooded in. The indefatigable Grimms composed grammar books and began work on a German dictionary so comprehensive, its last volume, Number 380 (*Wideit—Wiking*), was not completed until 1961. Their work can now easily be found on the Internet.

I have the feeling that for German poets and thinkers, it must have been bliss to be alive then. Philology was blooming, the field of Indo-European linguistics was founded, scholars of Sanskrit and Oriental studies were bent over their source texts, folk-tale collectors were swarming, and no language was too remote to be studied. Little by little, these researchers must have become aware that, although the old empire had long ago ceased to exist, the spirit of philology had unexpectedly and in all innocence transformed their country into a world power. Students came from all over Europe to their institutions of higher learning and those who couldn't make the pilgrimage to Göttingen or Berlin pored over the thick tomes from the imperial bookseller, the Realschulbuchhandlung, in Berlin, from Mohr und Zimmer in Heidelberg, or from Hirzel in Leipzig, in search of what they needed.

Thus irrupted a curious peoples' spring in the centre of Biedermeier Europe, ruled as it was by the calculations of great powers, the police and the censor. All of a sudden, no one wanted to be the distant province, protectorate, colony or pendant of an empire. All longed to become a real nation, sovereign and independent, with all the trappings: a flag, an anthem, their own bureaucratese, their own king or president. But how? The dreams from the barricades of 1789 had long since faded. It would be far cleverer to find another point of leverage. The French, the English, the Russians, all the established European states had a proper national culture. Their national languages dominated their academies, universities and conservatories whereas to rise to the higher strata of society in Norway you had to speak Danish, in Finland Swedish and in Estonia German, as if the natives had nothing to say. This situation had to change. The Germans had shown how it

was done: not with the barrel of a gun but with books in hand.

And so everyone followed the Brentanos' and the Grimms' example and started collecting their old songs, folk tales and sagas, composing dictionaries and grammars and showing the world that it had to reckon with this or that people, if not with a complete nation.

In Serbia, a farmer's son by the name of Vuk Karadžić, who had studied his Jacob Grimm, was anointed father of his fatherland. He fulfilled the entire programme on his own: he recorded oral traditions, wrote a large dictionary and codified Serbian grammar and spelling. In an opposite corner of Europe lived another farmer's son by the name of Ivar Aasen. He was an autodidact, which didn't hinder him from synthesizing Norway's dialects into the standardized language, New Norwegian, complete with a dictionary and an elaborated grammar. He wanted to present a worthy alternative to written and official Danish. Elias Lönnroth, whose mother tongue was Finnish despite his Swedish name, also came from humble origins. Herder was his guiding light. His self-appointed task was enormous: the first comprehensive dictionary, the usual collections of folk songs, sayings and riddles and, most importantly, a written version of the oral epic the *Kalevala*, taught to every schoolchild in Finnland. Lönnroth also invented many new words; no foreigners since his time understand words like *kirjallisuus* or *tasavalta*, that is, 'literature' and 'republic'. Swedish as a colonial language never quite recovered from Lönnroth's liberation struggle. Similar stories can be found in Lithuania and Latvia, and even Czech had to wait to come into its own for a scholar like Josef Dobrovský, the founder of Slavic Studies, and especially his student Josef Jungmann in the nineteenth century.

Unfortunately, however, we have to recognize that, as promising and successful as philology's triumphal march was, it ended just as spectacularly. What began as a movement of emancipation took a bloody turn over the following century and a half, ending in resentment, xenophobia and war. The vaunted right of nations to self-determination touted by ideologues as different as Vladimir Lenin and Woodrow Wilson continues to sow discord to this day. Recently the Kosovars and the South Sudanese managed to create their own nations. Others, like the Kurds, the Basque and the Scots are queuing up. And there is no end in sight.

The only one who sensed early on where this could lead was the polymath and clergyman in the Weimar court, Johann Gottfried Herder. 'National delusion,' he wrote, 'is a dreadful term. [. . .] He who does not concur is branded an idiot, an enemy, a heretic, an alien.' When asked what a nation is, he answered,

> A great, unweeded garden. Who would embrace this rallying place of foolishness and faults as well as sublimities and virtue without differentiating between them and take up arms against other nations? Obviously, it is the nature of things that individuals, like races and peoples must learn from and with each other until all have finally

understood the difficult lesson: no single people is God's chosen one on this earth; the truth must be sought by all and all must build the garden for the common good.

Very few are those who have heeded him.

RETIREMENT PLANS

No one has ever asked me what I think of retirement. I don't know my way around the labyrinthine tangles of labour, tariff, workplace and collective bargaining laws. This is because I belong to the miniscule minority of people who cannot be forced to retire. Such people have no 'employer' as legally defined. If you have never been hired, you cannot logically be fired.

Why, then, am I meddling in a discussion that, strictly speaking, doesn't concern me as I am neither 'an interested party' nor one of the experts who created the formula that determines a person's pension in Germany?

$$Rentemtl = E \; x \; Z \; x \; R \; x \; A$$

I have been informed that *Rentemtl* is the gross monthly pension in euros. *E* is the sum of compensation points, *Z* is the age factor at the time of retirement, *R* is the pension type factor, and *A* is the actual pension value in euros. I couldn't begin to say what compensation points are and I find the pension adjustment formula even more bewildering:

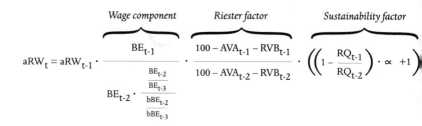

$$aRW_t = aRW_{t-1} \cdot \underbrace{\frac{BE_{t-1}}{BE_{t-2} \cdot \frac{\frac{BE_{t-3}}{bBE_{t-2}}}{bBE_{t-3}}}}_{\text{Wage component}} \cdot \underbrace{\frac{100 - AVA_{t-1} - RVB_{t-1}}{100 - AVA_{t-2} - RVB_{t-2}}}_{\text{Riester factor}} \cdot \underbrace{\left(\left(1 - \frac{RQ_{t-1}}{RQ_{t-2}}\right) \cdot \propto +1\right)}_{\text{Sustainability factor}}$$

Surely, I'm not alone here; millions of my fellow citizens must be as puzzled as I am. There is only one conclusion to be drawn: a solid majority of citizens are caught in a tight net of regulations they cannot understand. These directives are experienced as compulsion. This is hardly pleasant, but there is worse. There is reason to suspect that many people hate the jobs they do day in, day out, over decades. No one knows how many jobholders this applies to. Statistics on this fall short. Anyone relying on surveys must keep in mind that most of the answers given are untrue.

One thing is certain: many, perhaps even most jobs —to call them professions would be an overstatement— are rather dull, repetitive and without prospects. Medical insurance files show evidence of this. They contain accounts of depression and burn out, harassment and office politics.

Despite all this, secure employment is seen as protection against downward social mobility and poverty. It is, therefore, at once valued and loathed. The thought of finally turning one's back on the company, the administration, the factory or the office is an irresistible temptation for many weary people. They eagerly look forward to the day they can retire or receive their pension, even though their living situation as retirees will be relatively shabby—no one in their right mind believes any longer in the fairy-tale promise of a secure pension.

It is no surprise that government recommendations that the gainfully employed not only pay into 'private pension plans' above and beyond their social insurance contributions but also continue working for several additional years, fall on deaf ears.

This political agenda is a minefield. Long ago, probably in the 1960s, talk of reforms gave rise to optimistic visions. Today, however, it is considered threatening. Politicians who broach the topic put their re-elections at risk. They are well advised to wrap their plans in empty words and provisos and delay the effect of their resolutions until some distant day when they are no longer in office. This is not to say their reasons for acting are invented. On the contrary, they have been clear for decades.

The official system of retirement benefits was set up according to demographic projections made in the 1950s. Its basic principles date from that era. At the time, the average life expectancy in Germany was 71 years for women and 66 for men. Today it has risen to 83 years and 78 years respectively. Yet even these high averages are deceptive. In 2012, a 65-year-old could look forward to another 17 or 18 years before his time was up. There are many reasons for this: his cohort has been spared war, expulsion, imprisonment and starvation; medical care has improved significantly; obesity is replacing undernourishment; work hours have decreased and leisure time increased; people play sports, take holidays, get medical check-ups and watch their fitness and diet; and if these are not sufficient, therapists are consulted.

None of this, however, invalidates the biblical curse, *By the sweat of your brow . . .* It's no wonder that many rejoice at the prospect of fleeing the workplace—many, but not all. For every miner, patrol officer or roofer who is tired of his job, there's a masseur, cabinet maker or engineer who does not see why he should be forced to give up his work just because he has the bad luck to have reached retirement age. As strange as it may sound to the functionaries and committee chairmen, there are those who have no desire to spend the remainder of their lives pottering around the garden, on golf courses, or in a retiree ghetto in Spain. The defiant housekeeper who wants to keep cleaning houses to get out of her one-room apartment and supplement her tiny pension by working off the books is as much outside the bounds of the established regulations as the cancer researcher who emigrates to Norway or the United States because a German university has shown him the door.

They are strange people, indeed, who actually *like* their work! Who simply refuse to stop! Who fight tooth and nail to hold on to their jobs! On the one hand, these workers ruffle the workplace, defy 50-year-old pre-scriptions and leave themselves open to the charge of blocking younger workers from accessing positions. On the other hand, 'business' representatives complain and wring their hands over the difficulty of finding skilled professionals and vie for immigrants from all over the world because at home the next generation of workers can barely read, write or do maths.

If you ask me—but who on earth would consider asking me of all people—what is missing from the debate is a minimum of common sense. The standard employment history that committees dream of is a phantom, a chimera. Existing retirement age regulations are misleading. It is high time they were eliminated, even if it will cause the politicians more than a few sleepless nights.

There is a well-known rule of thumb in politics that the simpler and more reasonable a proposition, the harder it is to implement. There is no lack of examples illustrating this form of sabotage. It took decades to do away with the completely absurd law governing the opening hours of stores. Whether or not the absurdity of the German tax system will ever be corrected remains to be seen. Every attempt made in that direction is immediately and unanimously scotched by treasurers, subsidy recipients and interest groups.

It is thus extremely unlikely that one of the parties represented in the Bundestag will ever manage to offer a solution that serves both those who want to flee their jobs and those who want to keep them. Such a formula would have the disadvantage of being simple enough to fit on a beer coaster. It can be divided into two half-sentences. First: the elimination of all mandatory retirement-age restrictions. Second: restitution of freedom of contract.

In those circumstances, everyone could continue to work for as long as he or she wanted regardless of their date of birth provided all those and only those immediately concerned agree. The hypothetical roofer, therefore, would not have to work until he lands in the emergency room at 67, 69 or 70 years of age, as some number wizards prescribe. Nor would the over-energized workaholic have to defend his position as long as his boss and co-workers are willing to put up with him and he can do the job he is paid for.

This plan assumes, of course, that people differ from each other in ways that are not always easily understood—an assumption for which there is no room in the current system and which is foreign to any regulation of public misery. Nevertheless, a return to the conditions of the 1950s should remain a pipe dream. People were less intractable then. They worked in the factories and offices without complaint. When they were no longer wanted, they went home without complaint. Above all, they did the pension system the favour of going to the grave in a timely fashion.

SIX BILLION EXPERTS

For almost everything we cannot do, there are other creatures on the planet who seem able to do it with little effort. Some lichens can live to be a thousand without much trouble. Bacteria have solved the problem of reproduction, which causes many people no end of difficulty, with an enormously simple solution: divide in two and you're done. Birds navigate using the position of the sun, the polarization of light, and the earth's magnetic field. Butterflies have an enviably acute sense of smell.

No one knows how many species there are. The latest estimates are between seven and eleven million. Most have yet to be discovered, described and classified. But each of these species is breathtakingly specialized. Otherwise they wouldn't have survived. It is estimated that there are sixty to a hundred thousand different kinds of scorpion wasps buzzing around the earth. Some of them are hyperparasites, that is, they survive by attacking the larvae or pupae of other wasps, laying their eggs among them so their brood can feed on them. Jellyfish manage without a brain. Cyanobacteria create oxygen and sugars from sunlight, carbon dioxide and water, and exchange gene pools when necessary.

To be sure, it is always the species and not the individual that retains these highly developed faculties. Specialization follows a genetically fixed programme that can only be altered over the long term through variation and mutation. Scorpion wasps don't need to learn anything. The same is true for plants and animals. Neither horse enthusiasts nor dog lovers like to hear this. My stallion and my spaniel, they will say, are highly intelligent individuals, beyond compare to their untalented fellow species and most certainly to a jellyfish!

Such objections are not unreasonable. But they only mean that house pets have been bred, reared and trained for several millennia. They have no choice but to adapt to humans. And so the *canis familiaris* has learnt all sorts of tricks and become watchdog, tracking dog, sheepdog, guide dog, hunting dog, lap dog, sled dog, attack dog, etc.

A completely different kind of specialization has developed among social insects. One could describe it as a simple sort of division of labour. Each colony has at least one queen, the rest are workers; the males or drones serve only for reproduction. Perhaps it is because of this functional organization that ants are so successful and have a biomass that surpasses ours. No one doubts that their species will outlive us.

Nevertheless, we should not underestimate *Homo sapiens*. He is certainly not perfectly adapted to one specialty like the *Dolimochitus imperator* but has been forced by necessity to become an expert. He is a creature, as his Latin name indicates, who learns things by doing them, and not because evolution has programmed him to but on his own account and at his own risk. He cannot help but learn, and does so at a faster rate than the process of evolution which is in no hurry. This capacity for competence has no particular goal, no well-defined interest, and it is inherent in each exemplar of this extraordinary species. In fact, what is called the division of labour in society is but a tiny fraction of all that mankind does.

Accordingly, you could say the world is populated with some seven billion experts. Such a claim will no doubt invite objections. Does this number include people in coma or suffering from dementia? Does it include young children? Fine, to take the wind out of such objections' sails, we'll discount one seventh of the population. Even so, it was recently demonstrated that even 20-month-old babies are able to use computers skilfully. What about bores, untalented idiots, perennial failures? The answer is simple. Those who pursue that line of argument are taking the easy way out. Instead of limiting themselves to a quick glance, they should listen to each subject until their hidden expertise comes to light.

Officially recognized professions alone offer a fantastically vast field of activities. If you don't believe me, you should consult the *Index of Declared Occupations in Reports Filed with the National Insurance*. This work, compiled by a praiseworthy authority and sadly too little known, lists thousands of possible occupations over 366 pages. Each is given a code number and listed in alphabetical order from *Aalbrutzüchter* [eel fry breeder] to *Zytologieassistent* [cytotechnologist]. On the very first page the reader encounters such professions as *Abbeizer, Abbrecher, Abdichter, Abdreher, Abgrater, Ableger, Aböler, Abputzer, Abrechner and Abrichter* [paint remover, lapsed student, caulker, lathe worker, cameraman, removals, degreaser, cleaner, settlement clerk, trainer]. For the sake of political correctness, each one is followed by a slash and the feminine suffix *-in*.

But that is not all, not by a long shot. The concept of the division of labour is indispensable, yet it can easily be taken to absurd extremes. Most people's expertise is not restricted to the working world which, as we know, can be tedious indeed. It expands into the world of leisure where it flowers most exquisitely. No economist can measure the scope of this unremunerated work done without any thought of earnings, or fear of sacrificing time and money. In this obscure zone, collectors, in particular, hoard a wealth of bizarre knowledge and experiences. A German engineer responsible for the final inspection of jumbo jets in Toulouse, for example, developed a feverish interest in toys from the era of his childhood. He obviously no longer plays with his collection of delicate white plastic figurines of cows, trees, fences and such, all advertising a brand of margarine, but he does display them in his stairwell in a glass-fronted cabinet he built himself. He is also an authority on the Erdal shoe polish frog logo. He combs through all pertinent magazines, auction-house publications and catalogues to keep up to date. His passion more than compensates for the narrow field of his demanding professional career.

A laconic, tough-as-nails trucker from South Dakota who parked his rig outside the bar's front door reveals himself in conversation to be a hardcore opera fan. Not only does he know the repertoire, he is also familiar with the various recordings of each work and has an informed opinion about the performances of the respective soloists and conductors. As soon as the subject of the conversation changes, his interest evaporates and he sits silently, nursing his beer.

Certainly, there is an element of vice in such competencies. The dangers facing these private experts are obvious. How easily they can become dogmatists, pedants and bores! They are always at risk of slipping into fetishism. Furthermore, these enthusiasts have a penchant for flocking to clubs or Internet forums, which only exacerbates their obsessive tendencies. There is no lack of onlookers who deem such passions useless if not ridiculous. While a collector of contemporary art can and will bask in the glow of prestige, the owner of the foremost beer-coaster collection in the world will earn a few pitying smiles at best.

This is unjust because the question of usefulness is more difficult to decide than the extollers of profit believe. The Scottish archaeologist Harold J. Plenderleith wrote a definitive work on restoring damaged statues of antiquity. He invites us to reflect on how easily the smallest blemish on a torso can develop into a crater.

When asked how many readers he could expect for his book, he said: 'Maybe nine, maybe twelve. Of those who understand bronze disease, for example, there is one in Tokyo, one in Cairo, and perhaps a third in Texas. The rest is silence' There was an even smaller audience 150 years ago for the work of a modest Augustinian monk named Gregor Mendel, who was mostly interested in peas. He planted and crossbred this plant in the garden of his abbey in Brno. No one understood what he had in mind. Only after his death did it become clear that his work provided the first solid foundation for the new science of genetics.

It is difficult to predict what any expertise will yield. But what is even worse: they are morally neutral. The extraordinary talents of Samuel Cohen, the man who doggedly tinkered with the neutron bomb, can hardly be denied. The same goes for gifted con men, burglars, contract killers and torturers. This insight makes the praise for expertise stick in the throat of even the best-intentioned.

The discovery that humanity is a collection of unfettered experts can hardly please the well-paid and widely respected government and financial advisers, stock market gurus, and trend researchers and predictors who play an important role on boards, commissions, committees and in congresses and symposia, when they're not hosting talk shows. They may invoke science—through no fault of its own—as often as they'd like. But what will come of their authority if their monopoly begins to totter? They will have to share their privileged position with a few billion others who are as determined as they are to defend their hard-won territory. In the future, every madman and every sage will give everything he can do a try. It will be difficult to dissuade our species from following this risky recipe for success.

THE PITFALLS OF TRANSPARENCY

The secret is revealed. Pass it on!
Blurb, 2008.

The disenchantment of the world announced in the first year of First World War has made considerable progress since then. Conspiracy theories are one of its last victims. Those were times when many were convinced they knew who was to be blamed for everything: the Rosicrucians, the Illuminati, the Freemasons and the Jesuits. The eighteenth-century proponents of the Enlightenment were nothing short of zealous in their mission to expose these secret societies, as long as they were not members themselves.

One hundred years later, the search for a scapegoat for the plagues of capitalism took a less innocuous turn. *The Protocols of the Elders of Zion* proclaimed to a frightened world that Jews were now guilty of everything. And not only that: they wanted to control the world. This fabrication, redacted by the tsarist secret police in the early 1900s, seems to strike a chord as effectively today as it did then in the Arab world, in Russia, Japan and elsewhere.

The constant need for complots and conspiracies, both domestic and worldwide, has grown beyond measure. An entire industry feeds it with offerings that range from rumour-mongering to esotericism. The number of secrets ostensibly exposed is overwhelming. Depending on the search engine you prefer, your hunt for revelations will return 5 to 6 million hits. If you limit your search to conspiracy theories, you still have a choice of 3,900,000 entries.

The list of books in print reveals the extent and variety of the mysteries: not only the secrets of the calligrapher, the void, the cellist, the bicycle seller and the midwife, but also the Hamlet-, Midas-, swine flu-, Poseidon-, Methuselah- and diabetes conspiracies. Of course, there are also the usual suspects: the CIA, the Vatican and Wall Street. More productive than bookstores, of course, is the Internet, buzzing with talk of string pullers, back channels, secret societies and conspiracies. Hollywood also doesn't stint in its efforts to unmask the hidden machinations that hold sway over us all.

The media's aggressive promotion of thrillers lacks any hint of thrill, and the fervour with which *top secrets* are uncovered day in, day out shows that this societal model has reached a new stage.

What remains, however, are the *performative contradictions* inseparable from these revelations. This is what logicians call statements that refute themselves. If, for example, someone says that he is sleeping or is dead or is not saying a word, then he is disproving himself. It is the same for anyone proclaiming a purported secret in the market square. Rudolf Steiner, who published the book *An Outline of Occult Science* in 1910, had been struck by this antinomy. Fifteen years later, he had to defend himself against 'misunderstandings' the title had provoked. He was informed that a 'science' could not be 'occult'. He found the objection witless, as if someone who published a work on this topic wanted to keep it secret. Be that as it may, the old enchanter could not free himself from the trap he had laid.

These days, the market in secrets knows none of these scruples. The Enlightenment hope that man's lot would improve, the more darkness was illuminated, has become superfluous now that anyone who does not keep his eyes closed and ears covered is bombarded with information about everything that has happened, is happening, or might still happen. The excuse, once so useful and true, that one has never heard of this or that crime no longer has the slightest purchase.

And now interest, empathy and outrage are resources that are dwindling due to over-exploitation. Hardly anyone is able, these days, to understand or 'process' much less 'answer for' what he has been told. His powerlessness increases as the mass of information grows. It becomes clear that the hard-won freedom of the press, freedom of opinion and freedom of information have their dark sides which have only become clearer since the juggernaut of revelations overtook the classical print media. The initiative was taken by information technology, furthering the ability to gather data and instantly spread it around the world to extremes, making it accessible to anyone with a computer.

No government would want to do without this potential. Each nation carefully monitors its field of influence, surveys public spaces with cameras, taps telephones and searches computer files. Naturally, benevolent reasons are given for spying on the population; ultimately, it is a question of countering every danger, of fighting terrorism and organized crime, of protecting domestic industries from spies and of anticipating every possible threat. However, state agencies aren't the only eager ones on this front. 'Businesses' eavesdrop on their customers, the competition and their partners and hoard all the legal and illegal data they can get their hands on. The main product of these social networks is screening their members. This mass of personal information is the source of the phenomenal stock market value of Facebook and its rivals.

Society seems to have made its peace with the erosion of what used to be called the private sphere. The transparency gained with this development is self-evidently not limited to facts. Rumours, fabrications, denunciations and delusions are also welcome in the chaos of cyberspace. As a result, everyone who plays this game mutates into a hacker. The authorities investigate citizens, search engines consumers, the secret services their rivals, fraudsters bank accounts, China the Pentagon and vice versa and so on and so forth. In cyberwar, the victor is the one with the best software.

Just as in current military conflicts, asymmetrical warfare in cyberspace has gained ground. Guerrilla warriors who are difficult to apprehend go after well-guarded state secrets. An organization like WikiLeaks sees itself as a kind of meta-conspiracy that reveals war crimes to spectacular effect, behaving no differently than a group of conspirators.

The intelligence services are not the only ones to suffer from this flood of disclosures. The countless fiascos—they have only themselves to blame for—have eroded the public's sympathy. They have staged too many sordid farces for their own amusement. To this day, Fidel Castro boasts of the starring role he has played. How many times did American agents try to slip him an exploding cigar or a femme fatale with poisoned pills? Once they tried to destroy his beard with a depilatory chemical, then to make him go crazy with LSD or resorted to more traditional means like bombs, rifles and handguns. All for naught as everyone knows.

It is a characteristic of scandals and revelations that the more frequently they occur, the less serious the consequences. This applies not only to the backstairs politics of intelligence services but also more openly to cartel agreements and political donations, investment and subsidy fraud, insider trading and bribery, as well as tax evasion, money laundering, corruption and weapon trafficking. Each report of these activities is received with glee and just as happily forgotten. The average half-life of a scandal is three to four weeks.

Even the torture scenes in Abu Ghraib, visible at any time on YouTube, only led to prison terms for soldiers, including a six-month sentence for the one who took the photographs, while the higher-ups in the Pentagon remained unscathed. Private Bradley Manning is threatened with a more serious fate. The United States Army gave this poor devil, and 60,000 others, access to classified databases with information about numerous human rights violations perpetrated by the occupying forces in Iraq. Manning did not like what he saw and leaked the information to a contact at WikiLeaks, who made it public. He was threatened with a prison sentence of more than 50 years or, in the worst case, execution. [Manning is a transwoman, and is now known as Chelsea Elizabeth. Her 35-year sentence was commuted by President Barack Obama in January 2017.] The United States has announced its intent to withdraw from Iraq but otherwise little has changed. [The withdrawal was completed in 2011, but US troops were sent back in 2016.] Guantanamo remains a space without basic human rights. Abductions and targeted killings are in purview of 'special forces' in the United States and elsewhere.

The demand for complete transparency is no less ineffective in the civilian sphere. Corporations that have been fined millions for their malpractices pay from petty cash and continue business as usual. Even in America, the usual prison sentences which can theoretically exceed several hundred years, have no apparent deterrent effect. Convicted hedge fund managers can count on a comfortable cell in which they can wait for early release before heading off to Singapore or elsewhere to start a new investment firm. In the industries responsible for one financial crisis after another, firms continue their work undisturbed, as if they had never been 'exposed'.

Even the practices of international politics differ little from this basic pattern, as is obvious from the frequency with which treaties are violated in the European Union. Jean-Claude Juncker expressed it clearly when serving as Chairman of the Eurogroup: 'We reach a decision, communicate it clearly, and wait to see what happens. When there are no cries of objection and no revolts, because most people don't understand what has been decided, then we press on, step by step until there is no turning back.'

Political lies have long been a realpolitik necessity with regard to the all-powerful financial markets. The fact that they are short-lived and very soon disproven renders them a kind of *acte grauit*. It's merely a matter of delaying the confutation until after the next election. Here, too, public outrage is limited.

Still, the positive side is not hard to find, there are plenty of examples. It is easier than ever before, we are told, *to hold one of the great secrets in the universe in your hands. It has been passed down through the century to you. This is the secret to everything—joy, health, wealth, relationships, love, happiness . . . everything you could wish for. All this for the first time in human history.* If this is not enough for you, the bonus material that will give a look behind the scenes. Rated for viewers 6 years old and above, the movie that promises so much consolation was released by Spirit Movie Editions as *The Secret*. It won't set you back much—a mere $9.99 online.

It's hard to imagine a more beautiful flowering of the performative contradiction. But even the few pages you've just read aren't exempt from it. That a secret's value falls to zero with the hyperinflation of disclosure is a fact that can as easily be met with silence as brought to light.

POOR ORWELL!

A far-sighted man, that Eric Blair, who was better known under the pseudonym George Orwell. He knew a thing or two about totalitarian regimes before the concept became part of the historian's lingo. He foresaw the superpowers' antagonism and the Cold War when Stalin, Churchill and Roosevelt met in Tehran in 1943.

A few years after the Second World War, he published his famous novel, *1984*. Orwell did not like the future he saw coming. He painted a panoramic picture of a reign of terror that would refine the methods and ideologies of Hitler and Stalin in the middle of Europe in the foreseeable future: with a one-party system led by a 'Big Brother', a controlled language called 'Newspeak' that removes all complexity from language, the eradication of the private sphere, total surveillance, re-education and indoctrination of all citizens, with an all-powerful secret police whose task it is to eliminate every oppositional movement through torture, imprisonment in concentration camps and murder.

Fortunately for him and our part of the world, George Orwell's prophecy was wrong. He never would have dreamt that some of those goals, especially total surveillance of citizens, would be possible without recourse to violence, that no dictatorship would be necessary for them to be realized, that even a democracy could meet them through civil, if not pacifist, means.

These means had been described more than 400 years ago by young Frenchman. In his essay *The Discourse on Voluntary Servitude*, Étienne de la Boétie, that was his name, was not content to pillory the absolute rulers of his time. Most importantly, he appealed to the consciences of those who accommodated themselves to tyranny. It is the people themselves, he wrote, who

> permit, or, rather, bring about their own subjection, since by ceasing to submit they would put an end to their servitude. A people enslaves itself, [. . .] gives consent to its own misery, or, rather apparently welcomes it. [. . .] Do not imagine that there is any bird more easily caught by decoy, nor any fish sooner fixed on the hook by wormy bait, than are all these poor fools neatly tricked into servitude by the slightest feather passed, so to speak, before their mouths.

Yet we haven't had to be concerned about such individual tangible and assailable monarchs as La Boétie was protesting against. It is no Orwellian Big Brother who rules us but a system like the one Max Weber described in the 1920s:

> [B]ureaucratic organization, with the assignment of its functions to a multitude of specialized experts, its rigid regulation of competence

and its hierarchical pattern of obedience to the respective superior authority [. . .] is, together with the lifeless machinery, about to produce the iron cage of future serfdom in which men will have to live helplessly, like the fellahin in ancient Egypt, if they consider an efficient, that is to say, rational, bureaucratic administration which also provides for their needs, as the only and ultimate ideal that is to determine the nature of their own government.

Weber called this new enslavement an 'iron cage' but this lucid thinker did not see quite clearly. For this cage has become a relatively comfortable pen, resembling rather a padded room. Our keepers tread softly in rubber-soled shoes. They work to reach their primary strategic goals, seamless surveillance and the eradication of the private sphere, as noiselessly as possible. Only when there is no alternative do they reach for the cudgel. They prefer to remain anonymous. They wear no uniforms but suits and ties. They have titles like Manager or Commissioner and do their jobs in air-conditioned offices instead of barracks. At work, they appear benevolent, offering the inmates security, assistance, comfort and nourishment. Accordingly, they can count on the occupants' silent consent and can be confident their charges will push the invisible button labelled 'Like'.

Another point in Weber's analysis seems anachronistic today. His sincere faith in the state's competence and efficacy is foreign to us, and not just because the global financial markets drive governments. Neither Berlin, nor Brussels, nor Washington would be able to exert complete control over their citizens on their own. Their functionaries are simply too helpless and not skilled enough. Nor do they have adequate technological mastery. The authorities, therefore, are dependent on 'business', that is, on international firms in the IT industry. Only when both sides, governments and companies like Google, Microsoft, Apple, Amazon and Facebook, work hand in hand does a pincer grip on freedom have any chance of great success. It's clear that in these fragile alliances political authorities play the role of a junior partner. Only the corporations have at their disposal the necessary expertise, the necessary capital and the necessary factotums: computer scientists, engineers, software developers, hackers, mathematicians and cryptographers.

In the twentieth century, the Gestapo, the KGB and the Stasi couldn't have dreamt of such technological capacities: ubiquitous surveillance cameras, automatic monitoring of telephone and electronic communication, high-definition satellite pictures, detailed motion profiles, biometric facial recognition, all the programs guided by amazing algorithms and stored in data banks with unlimited memory capacity.

The last movement protesting the German authorities' and the corporations' zeal occurred a long time ago and is nearly forgotten. In 1983, a year before Orwell's date, a relatively harmless census caused an uproar. A surprisingly large number of citizens called on the Federal Constitutional Court and their complaints were successful. Karlsruhe decided against the government's actions and even stipulated a new fundamental right to 'informational self-determination' to protect personality rights, a judgement that today seems naive. No one has respected it. In the cyberwar against the general population, the powerless protectors of data threw in the towel long ago.

George Orwell was certainly right about the regulation of language. His Newspeak has become an official sociolect. The so-called services do not care for the constitution and their activity is difficult to distinguish from that of computer criminals. The new 'bill of health' is in fact an electronic medical file that is easy prey for any experienced hacker and the 'social networks' take advantage of their users' exhibitionism by exploiting it mercilessly.

Cash is one final irritating residue of the private sphere. It's only logical that the state would work concertedly with corporations to eliminate it. Proliferating credit and loyalty cards serve to their advantage. Further, chip and remote payment methods will soon be widespread. The point of it all is unmistakable: the most complete monitoring possible of all transactions. The tax authorities are as interested as the 'asocial' networks, online commerce, the credit industry, advertising and the police. Additionally, all memory of money as a material object will be eradicated, reduced to an arbitrarily manipulable piece of data.

For the sake of completeness, let's take a look at a minor theatre of operation in the media: the attempt to get rid of copyright. This was a relatively recent achievement, dating from the nineteenth century. Until then, reading books remained a privilege accorded to a small minority. When the novel became a product sold on a large scale, authors realized they could make real money once they had a share from editions and translations. Their joy, unfortunately, didn't last long. Today printed books are considered discontinued models and, therefore, many consider copyright to be a nuisance to the glee of the digital avant-garde. These happy pirates feel that paying for what the IT industry calls content is absurd. Those previously called authors are meant to work for free and for that they can tweet, chat and blog to their heart's content. No one seems to be bothered by the fact that the half-life of available computer technology, according to IT company market cycles is between three and five years. Whereas a text on parchment or acid-free paper can still be read easily after 500 to 1,000 years, electronic media have to be updated and recopied often in order to be accessible after one or two decades. That, of course, is in line with the intentions of those in control.

The elimination of printed books is hardly a new idea. It was first floated a long time ago. Ray Bradbury, presented it in his 1953 bestseller(!) *Fahrenheit 451* along with its far-reaching consequences. In his utopian novel, the possession of a book is a capital crime. Great pessimists tend to exaggerate in their visions of the future.

Yet, the fact that their visions did not come true cannot be held against them. Instead, it is to their credit. This applies to Bradbury as well as to Orwell or Max Weber. Being smarter in hindsight is no great achievement.

As unavoidable as the *Amen* in church is the question we must ask of each bleak prognosis: Is there any positive aspect to this outlook? The answer is easy. It is extremely gratifying to note that our voluntary servitude has, to date, been brought about without any bloodshed. The 'remnants of history' have not been liquidated as Lenin had demonstrated in Russia. The reason is obvious. Our overseers' tolerance is based on a simple cost-benefit calculus. The cost of eliminating the last traces of resistance increase astronomically the closer the ideal state of affairs. A 95 per cent surveillance rate is satisfactory. Eliminating the small, but stubborn minority opposed to the promises of the digital era out of sheer obstinacy would be prohibitively expensive. Nonetheless, 5 per cent of the German population is more than 4 million people. Therefore: no need to panic! Today and in the future, those who refuse to accept the digital era can, happily continue eating and drinking, loving and hating, sleeping and reading unobserved—if they do so analogically.

THE DELIGHTFUL DISPLEASURES
OF CULTURE

No one can deny that Germany has a cultural life. The doubts about its existence that are raised now and again are not to be taken seriously. This cultural life is not a phenomenon that is merely tolerated—it is universally recognized and widely supported. For it to flower, the federal government, the federal states and municipalities, with the support of foundations, sponsors and patrons of the arts, hand out considerable sums of money. Even the welfare state agrees—it includes participation in the arts of children and adolescents as part of a subsistence level existence and, therefore, gives recipients of benefits 10 euros a month for every child, although this sum is also expected to cover sports-club membership fees.

This alone demonstrates how impossible it is to define the domain of cultural life. The number of participants is unknown. Any attempt to calculate it would be like trying to nail pudding to the wall. Nevertheless, the number of artists applying for social security does offer some indication. These statistics conscientiously categorize those insured by profession, sex and age. In the section 'literary arts', there are, we're told, 42,038; in the visual arts 59,684; in music 46,394; in the performing arts 21,546; for a total of 169,662 active ladies and gentlemen. Other sources give a figure as high as 320,000 'artists and associated professionals'. That's not bad if you consider that this is only a subset. Above and beyond those listed are the countless people concerned with administering and managing the operations. They are all, from the doorman to the general manager, from the receptionist to the cultural attachés, from the museum guard to the minister, for the most part permanent employees, salaried positions with benefits, which cannot be said for artists. Institutions of higher learning offer courses of study and degrees to prepare new generations of cultural administrators.

It's impossible to count the number of events, festivals, openings and launches, concerts, exhibitions and symposia offered day after day in every corner of the country. Even more impressive is the enormous number of people in our republic who gather to enjoy these cultural fruits. Still, care is taken to keep their delight within bounds. Cultural life, after all, is not only varied—it also takes effort. Many of the musical offerings include ear-splitting noise. There are endless theatre productions and readings that one fears will never end. Those sitting in the middle of the row will have a hard time escaping. Blockbuster exhibits, the pride of all museums, try the visitors' patience before they even reach the door. After they've finally made it through the queue, they find themselves in a dense crowd of people that blocks their view of what they'd come to see. Getting a hold of opera tickets can require as bitter a struggle. Rock concerts in a field often end in mud. The press for the improvised toilets require an enormous stamina for standing, and hungry spectators who brave the concession-stand queues may arrive at the counter only to find the kitchen has closed.

Those are simply trivial matters, one might object, and never have any lasting deterrent effect. It's far more stimulating to ask what the interested public is offered and why.

This is not a new question. It dates from the dawn of the Modern Age in Paris, the capital of the nineteenth century. That's when the rules, oddities and complicated manoeuvring now characteristic of relations between artists and the public were invented. Almost all of them originated in France. In *Scènes de la vie de bohème*, Henri Murger popularized a lifestyle that presented the artistic world as a symbolic countervailing power to bourgeois society. Legendary figures like Arthur Rimbaud and Paul Verlaine embody this stance. *Épater la bourgeoisie* was a slogan directed not only at the mores and conventions of the Quartier Latin but also at the formal aspects of art. Scandal and provocation became the preferred mode and soon were an entrée into the avant-garde. Naturally, it was no accident that the aggression was directed against the bourgeoisie. This was the only social class that paid them any attention. The labourers and farmers had other things on their minds.

Yet German philosophy was not asleep. In 1853, it had already produced an *Aesthetics of Ugliness*, a catchword the artists could not resist. The brave author had sensed that there was a certain 'pleasure in ugliness'. He noted further that 'torn spirits feed on ugliness, since it becomes for them in a way the ideal of their negative state.' At roughly the same time, the phrase *nostalgie de la boue* began making the rounds in Paris, signifying a discreet decadent longing for degradation.

These artistic strategies were extremely successful as long as they met with furious resistance. For decades, their initiates' imaginations were fired by the hope for scandal, for prosecution and the incomprehension on the part of most of their fellow citizens.

With time it became clear that the despised bourgeoisie had a strong stomach indeed. They became ever-more inured to the forbidden fruits and learnt to delight in them, leaving only the ignorant and Johnny-come-latelys to object to the impertinences of the avant-garde. The bourgeoisie's shrugging tolerance must have annoyed the artists no end. There was nothing left for the latter to do but up the ante. Two famous propositions from 1930 are exemplary of this trend: 'The simplest Surrealist act consists of dashing down into the street, pistol in hand, and firing blindly, as fast as you can pull the trigger, into the crowd . . . The justification of such an act is, to my mind, in no way incompatible with the belief in that gleam of light that Surrealism seeks to detect deep within us'. Nothing helped, not even raising the stakes. After the Second World War, there were ever more signs of fatigue. New labels like *Neo-Avant-garde* or *Postmodern* had to be created. The art market eagerly swallowed up all works that had a tang of subversion. In 2008, nine André Breton handwritten notebooks which included his first manifesto, were sold at auction by Sotheby's for the record price of 3,626,250 euros. It became harder and harder to be controversial. Not only Picasso's popularity but also Andy Warhol's increased immeasurably. Artists longed desperately, and in vain, for bourgeois they could unmask. The prices they could rake in for their audacity, like investment bankers' bonuses, rose even during the financial crisis.

In 1966, a renowned Austrian writer's play *Publikumsbeschimpfung* [Offending the Audience] was greeted with a storm of applause and praise from spectators and critics alike. Since then season subscribers to state-supported theatre, like the ministries that support them, have shown a patience of saints without historical precedent. Theatre audiences are no longer outraged if someone urinates on a crucifix or engages in intimacies on stage. Of course, this alarming complaisance only encourages the directors' sadistic inclinations.

Also, the traditional separation of high- and low-brow culture has not kept pace with the freedoms won in the last century. On the one hand, the so-called New Music's ban on melody accustomed audiences to the onslaught of shrill torments they have even come to welcome. The bad listening habits of old are routinely broken and despised traditional recipes are done away with. Yet fans of rock and pop music are not spared their own trials. Gangsta rap, techno beats and heavy metal basses are not only aimed at the ears but also the gut, following the motto: Praised be that which makes us hard.

Just as peculiar as the public's enthusiasm is crush of those who are willing to meet it. This may have to do with a wish that many starting out in the workplace have: to avoid the boredom that awaits them (which is the case in many jobs). Or is it connected to the widespread urge for self-fulfilment? Whatever it is— now as in the past, cultural life exerts a powerful attraction. And it does so even though it offers little more than exploitative working conditions. Badly paid interns, when they're paid at all, and volunteers are the rule, rather than the exception in a cultural industry that can always tap a small reserve army. The average salary of a 'creative' is below that of a postman. Unemployment rates are high. The risk of poverty in old age is known. And yet, the entire cultural sphere enjoys a cachet that is difficult to understand. 'One day, I'll make it big'—is an idea people cling to. All warnings about the difficulty of cultural life founder on this promise which lures a sympathetic public as well as the fearless seeking fortune into this milieu. One can't wish them more than great tenacity and even greater luck.

There is certainly no lack of grouchy onlookers steeped in cultural pessimism; yet in our land preaching doom and gloom will never give them the upper hand or get them much notice.

AS IF

The largest German aeronautical corporation owns a series of simulators in Frankfurt am Main. The enormous machines are elevated on stilts and look like the nose of a cargo plane. Twice a year every pilot has to undergo a training programme there that functions as an exam. The candidate sits in the cockpit next to an experienced aircraft captain facing a frightening array of measuring instruments, controls and flickering screens. An arbitrary location on earth is given as the goal. The windows display accordingly Alpine peaks, the Shanghai skyline or the Nile Delta. An impressive sight, to be sure, but much more decisive are the runway and landing-strip markings.

The simulator can alternate between daylight, twilight and night, and can summon sandstorms and rain or snow showers. Turbulence, engine fires and near misses can occur at any time. Emergency landings and hijackings are also part of the programme. The trainee's adrenaline level spikes from the career risk he runs should he fail even though he knows he will walk out of the cockpit unharmed.

For technology freaks, simulated flight is a delicacy. But even philosophers who have no idea how to fly a plane can reap a sweet reward from such a test. The French writer Jean Baudrillard, who was the height of fashion 30 years ago, would no doubt have been completely taken with it. At the time, he insisted that simulation had replaced reality. In a furious bout of washing up, he also heralded the disappearance of the subject, history, the social, criticism and desire. According to him, for example, the Gulf War had never taken place. Hundreds of seminar papers appeared in his wake, and according to Baudrillard's logic, it's plausible to wonder if they or their writers ever truly existed. After all, since there was no longer any difference between being and seeming, every simulation would not only be moot, all the academic contortions about the topic would be invalid.

In reality, the word *simil* means nothing more than similar. To simulate means to make something similar. The result of the action is a *simulacrum*. That is what the ancients called their idols two and a half millennia ago: images of their gods. Because the gods did not show themselves, images were created and worshipped. All the peoples of the ancient Orient were familiar with such embodiments. Some of these statues were said to be able to speak; it was believed they could move and predict the future. In that regard, they belong to the early history of automatons. But were the gods actually present or was their presence mere appearance? This question has long preoccupied believers. In some religions, sacred images are venerated to this day; in others, they are proscribed. For suspicion grew with the doubt they inspired. The golden calf was toppled and the arts of the temple priests suddenly seemed mere mummery. Since then *simulatio* has also meant 'an assumption, false show, feigning, shamming'.

In the seventeenth century, a new figure appeared: the simulant. In Molière's *Imaginary Invalid*, audiences thought they were seeing a man who was dissimulating, who was 'only acting as if'. But the case is more complicated than it seems. In his famous clinic, the Salpêtrière, Jean-Martin Charcot proved that hysterics, as they were then called, could present authentic symptoms. A recent medical textbook states that many clinical pictures can be imitated exactly, for example, some patients have very skilfully simulated the clinical presentation of a heart attack. Another philosopher, Hans Vaihinger, a mostly forgotten Neo-Kantian, conceptualized the problem in his main work, *The Philosophy of 'As If'*. The title is, indeed, the most inspired bit of this 800-page long, dry-as-dust tome.

Nietzsche had already written that the human machine must be powered by illusions. Who is not aware that every society, like each one of us, is equipped with more or less artful delusions? That said, it's not always easy to distinguish between delusion and self-delusion. Without what economists call the 'money illusion', reserve banks would have to pack it in. Yet delusion is not just a necessity, it's also a game in which disbelief is intentionally suspended. 'The world wants to be deceived'—this saying from the Renaissance is patently ambiguous. It refers not only to the actions of tricksters, prestidigitators, and con men but also to a desire that art has exploited from the beginning.

A famous Greek legend recorded by Pliny attests to this ambiguity:

> In a contest between Zeuxis and Parrahasius, Zeuxis produced so successful a representation of grapes that birds flew up to the stage-buildings where it was hung. Then Parrahsius produced such a successful *trompe-l'oeil* of a curtain that Zeuxis, puffed up with pride at the judgement of the birds, asked that the curtain be drawn aside and the picture revealed. When he realized his mistake, with an unaffected modesty he conceded the prize, saying that whereas he had deceived birds, Parrhasius had deceived him, an artist.

So it is with the trompe-l'oeil tradition that flourished in the seventeenth and eighteenth centuries. The distance that separates optical illusion from forgery is no greater than that between illusion and disillusion. The most recent scandals in the art world show how the two overlap. When a forger is 'unmasked', the public is fascinated by his skill and delights in his 'coup' of being able to paint *as if* he were Max Ernst or Picasso.

Every act of simulation raises the question of 'genuineness', of 'authenticity'. The more successful a forgery is, the more we want to be deceived. Not by chance did the Grimm brothers associate the word *Finte* [feint] etymologically with the Latin words *fictio* and *simulatio* in their dictionary of the German language. They even add *machine*, which almost brings us full circle to *simulator*. Only a very astute philosopher of language would be able to analyse the entire semantic field of such expression as 'I imagine that . . . ', 'I'm acting as if . . . ', 'I'm pretending . . . ', 'I let myself be convinced . . . ', 'I figure . . . ', etc.

Old categories like sensory illusion or sham have been replaced by the concept of virtuality, which even the exact sciences use. Luckily these scientists don't restrict themselves to postmodern jargon. They usually know exactly what they're talking about. It has always been so. For Lucretius, who lived in the first century BCE, *simulacra* were no longer idols to be worshiped but natural phenomena, images that we have created following the teachings of Democritus and Epicurus, of atoms and of the manifold changing shapes of clouds.

In mathematics, however, the concept of simulation only appeared two thousand years later. Here, success does not depend on subjective criteria or skill but on models one has created. Without computers, it would be impossible to complete the calculations necessary for sophisticated probabilities. Every weather forecast shows clouds that do not exist but whose formation can be predicted with a certain degree of likelihood. Although weather forecasts are not certain, we trust them enough to pack warm clothes and an umbrella. Demographers follow the same system when warning politicians of the possible financial burden of future pensions, as do actuaries when assessing risks of catastrophes.

The most ambitious simulations have created a field of research that calls itself artificial intelligence. Nevertheless, even the thickest numbskull wouldn't confuse the modest achievements of artificial intelligence with the natural intelligence of a dog or a raven. Still, there are many applications of simulation that have dropped from the stratosphere of theory into everyday life. Computer games have become a worldwide addiction and few of the larger film productions could be completed without computer-generated images.

At the same time, however, anyone who sees one of those films or follows a weather forecast knows what to expect. No one, except perhaps Jean Baudrillard, confuses the *As If* with *As Is*. We are practised in playing with the ambiguity in which illusion and disillusion are held in the balance. That balancing act is characteristic of the way we deal with such technology.

I said earlier that anyone who wishes to play the pilot can do so in the Frankfurt flight simulator. An experienced aircraft captain and two hours of training are included in the price. To steer a plane that weighs 350 tonnes at takeoff is no small feat. And yet, the amateur in the cockpit is told that, with luck, even the clueless can stick the landing. Should he fail, at least the damage will be contained. Despite his cold sweat, he will land the plane successfully after that trip. He gladly let himself be fooled but that he was simultaneously flying and had his feet on the ground was never in doubt. This double-consciousness is the charm at the heart of every simulation.

WHITHER PHOTOGRAPHY?

Our perception depends on the media that we use—and that use us. This is nothing new. What we understand as a 'landscape' only existed after painting presented it to us. Without the telescope, we would have no double stars and without the microscope, no bacteria.

Yet another medium has affected our ability to see the world far more than framed paintings: photography. It's difficult—it's almost impossible—for us to imagine how our forebears perceived their surroundings before the camera existed. The camera is our omnipresent and insatiable third eye.

Its lens has captured things great and small as well as things too ordinary and insignificant to have caught our attention without the camera's interference. The beauty particular to tools and machine parts was invisible to most until it was revealed by the school of New Objectivity, of which Albert Renger-Patzsch was a great master. We saw nature differently too, once we had the example of Karl Blossfeldt's abstract plant forms. This type of photography blossomed during the Weimer

Republic, although it was hardly its invention as the photographs of Eugène Atget and Edward Steichen show. It can be traced all the way back to the nineteenth century when natural scientists were among the first to seize upon photography and in turn, the camera revolutionized their research in astronomy as well as in biology and medicine. The historian of science, Lorraine Daston, charted this phenomenon in her ground-breaking study.

On the whole, it's clear that without Henry Fox Talbot, Nicéphore Nièpce, Louis Daguerre and their successors, what we see today would look different to us than it does. This is not because of the little rectangular pictures we keep in our wallets and albums. Far beyond its origins, photography became the mother of all modern visual media, from film and TV to the new imaging techniques stalking our brains.

Many intelligent people have worked hard to compile a conclusive theory of this leading medium, to conceptualize it, so to speak. Did they succeed? If we look at the insights offered to us by Walter Benjamin, Roland Barthes, Susan Sontag and many other incisive minds, we are justified in expressing some doubt. For photography breaks all the rules, overflows all definitions and, almost two hundred years after its first appearance, continues to engender new forms of perception, art and surveillance. It is difficult to find a denominator common to all its protean transformations. Thus, anyone thinking about photography will sooner or later get lost in a media labyrinth. Photography is many things at once:

propaganda, art, advertisement, aerial reconnaissance, fashion show, satellite surveillance, reportage, pornography, fetish, commemoration, espionage, scientific documentation, court evidence . . . Every attempt to describe it founders on its metamorphoses—as do these lines.

Photography freed itself long ago from visible light and conquered other wavelengths on the light spectrum: infrared and UV, X-rays, magnetic resonance and scintigraphy. Photography now also shows us the invisible. Astrophysicists no longer sees stars but false colour images generated by a computer, just as doctors are not faced with organs but with screens, and high energy physicists assess traces of particles delivered by his detector. These offer strange counterparts to the naive snapshots immortalized in family albums and the postcards that dictate what sights are worth seeing!

One might wonder where the millions of snapshots end up that capture moments of holidays, weddings or football games. In boxes and drawers? On discs? In archives? In the garbage dump? Digitalization has increased their number astronomically although a merciful trick of technology allows us to permanently delete them.

Facebook, Google and other Internet colossuses with unlimited storage capacity do not avail themselves of this option. Whatever they collect, they keep. Driven by complex algorithms, their data banks are the commercial descendants of the civil registers used to monitor the population since the nineteenth century. The fruits of this police work are the mug books, dactyloscopy and the passport photograph. In our time surveillance has reached another level with omnipresent security cameras, DNA analysis and new biometric techniques. This boundless dossier is supplemented with voluntary contributions from innumerable amateur paparazzi, holding their smartphones up wherever anything is 'happening': a catastrophe, a crime, a revolution, a sporting event, a criminal hearing, a pop concert . . . The only ones who are not watched are those who hole themselves up inside their own four walls, that is, at least as long as no intelligence service takes an interest in them.

Photography is manipulation. It would be pointless to use that as a reproach. Lighting and exposure, cropping and backdrops, retouching and magnification are photographic techniques that were used by pioneers of the art form. The ateliers' clientele were never so naive as to think the palm trees in the background were real. How much of any shot is 'authentic' and how much is part of the staging is something the viewer must decide in each case. He can't pretend he's not aware that everything the camera delivers can be dismembered, disassembled, recombined, erased and falsified. What once only experts and tinkerers were in a position to do can now be accomplished at home by anyone who has access to a computer and the appropriate software.

Everything that can possibly be done has been done already. David King offers memorable proof of this in his book *The Commissar Vanishes*. In it, he documents the official Stalinist practice of erasing all traces of certain people as political constellations shifted. Such obvious manipulations occur most frequently during armed conflicts. Kipling had noted that truth is the first casualty of war. But there are more subtle ways of instrumentalizing the truth. Which part of a photograph is authentic might not be at all clear. In fact, since it is a medium that does not in principal distinguish between the original and a copy, 'authenticity' is a problematic concept in photography. Other artistic genres share its precarious relation to the truth.

As Marshall McLuhan showed us half a century ago, new media rarely do away with their predecessors. Accordingly, the once-widespread misconception that photography had killed off painting has faded. From the beginning, these two art forms have been in an uneasy relationship. The great masters of painting have used cameras to their own ends and in return photography has been guided by the visual arts. There is a movement in contemporary painting that calls itself Photorealism. Even obsolete media like the polaroid survive their extinction in art.

Coloured drawings still compete successfully with photography in anatomy textbooks and botanical guides. This is due to the fact that a photograph can only show one specimen, not the type. Here again the idea of objectivity begins to wobble. Sometimes a graphic abstraction can teach more than the close observation of a concrete individual case.

The question of whether or not photography is an art form no longer keeps anyone awake at night. Its paradoxes are all the more evident for its acceptance as one of the visual arts. Its most intelligent practitioners reflect on them in their work. David Hamilton, Andreas Gursky or Gerhard Richter are among the most accomplished practitioners of this. Nicholas Kahn and Richard Selesnick have reconstructed historical settings that look deceptively like 'authentic' shots. Another artist painstakingly creates for his camera forest landscapes that never existed. Works that highlight their own transitoriness, like most of Christo and Jeanne-Claude's installations, depend on photography for their survival.

Photography's breathtaking career in the art market ultimately raises an entire series of questions and not just about the problem of artificially created rarity. Of course, many historical photographs are unique copies. At auction, a heliograph or a calotype from the early nineteenth century will garner fantastically high bids. As a general rule, old photographs possess a particular dignity that is hard to explain. You could almost call it an aura. This is not true of contemporary photographs that can be reproduced identically at will.

This practice has its origins in older media. As long as there has been an art market, copperplate engravers and etchers have been focused on exclusivity to increase the value of their works. Printing plates were often destroyed even before the quality of the prints deteriorated. The destruction served the printers' speculations.

Later, artists began numbering and signing approved prints. Nevertheless, the concept of vintage prints brings a certain piquancy to photography by flouting the medium to which it is applied.

Ever since art has been called art, which has been the case, of course, for only a few centuries, doubt has followed it like its own shadow. Even when painting alone ruled the art trade, the question of the original was not free from bitter controversy. There have always been swarms of replicas, copies, false attributions and lamentable as well as superb forgeries. It is tempting to subscribe to Andy Warhol's dispassionate and succinct conclusion: *Art is what you can get away with*. Yet today as in the past, viewers should not let themselves be duped but keep another maxim in mind: The more fool he who trusts the art market more than his own eyes.

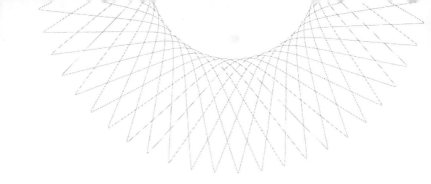

ORDINARY MIRACLES

God created everything from nothing,
But the nothingness shows through.

Paul Valéry

We have grown used to crises. You don't need to read a newspaper or to turn on the TV to find news of the latest calamities. It has dogged our steps for years, ever since we began carrying little mobile alarms with us wherever we go. Daunted by incomprehensible catastrophes and pursued by niggling worries, we live in a normalcy riddled with holes through which Chaos leers at us.

We have become accustomed to the fact that something will always go wrong: our flight is cancelled, the call centre answers only with lift muzak, the escalator is broken, the highway closed. Everywhere we look there are no-parking zones, stock market and computer crashes, football hooliganism, tornados, rent increases, holes in the ozone, traffic jams and asymmetrical wars. The TV news swings bewilderingly between the momentous and the insignificant. The muddle irritates and confuses but it doesn't surprise us. Those who read poetry have heard it from Rilke: To endure is all.

But that's only half of the truth. What would the other half look like if we tried a new point of view for a change? What if we asked ourselves how it is that anything ever comes off smoothly? Instead of complaining about all the things that go wrong, we should be astonished that in the midst of the insanity one thing or another actually works and not just occasionally or exceptionally but day in, day out.

In this our mundane reality violates the second law of thermodynamics, which states that any system inevitably tends towards entropy; in other words, towards disorder. It sounds more mysterious than it is. That is to say, maximum disorder is at the same a maximal equalizing of all differences, also called heat death. When this state is reached, nothing more can happen. There are no disruptions, which means there are no signs of life. Of course, we would no longer exist and, therefore, could no longer get upset.

However, even this inviolable law has a catch. It only applies to *isolated* systems. Where, actually, are these to be found? Take the universe, to choose a particularly large example, is it closed off and isolated? No one knows for certain, though it is possible. Nevertheless, no one can claim that the earth is a closed system because the sun provides radiation energy until it has burnt itself out. Until that happens in a few billion years, we should be patient and accept three things. First: All spontaneously occurring processes are irreversible. Second: There are no systems that will not break down sooner or later. And yet a third: What is truly miraculous is not that this or that collapses, but that many systems maintain at least a precarious balance for a period of time. To be sure, they are always close to the tipping point, but anyone living in such circumstances is convinced things will go on a good while yet. For example, you're waiting at the corner bus stop and a miracle occurs—the bus actually comes. You enter the nearest supermarket and the bottle of fresh milk is ready and waiting. You cross the street and there's no sound of machine-gun fire. The doorbell rings and it's not the KGB, the Office of the Protection of the Constitution or the mafia but your usual package courier, as reliable and good-humoured as ever.

We call these circumstances normal, although they're anything but a given. To appreciate this, all you need is a minimum of historical and geographical knowledge. Here, in Germany, a time of absolute horror lies just a few decades behind us and in other countries it is the order of the day now as in the past. There life is often, in the words of the English philosopher Thomas Hobbes, 'poor, nasty, brutish and [. . .] short'. What we see when we look out the window or step outside our door is an exceptional phenomenon—extremely unlikely and difficult to explain.

How are 'orderly circumstances'—whatever that means—at all possible in a society composed in no small part of freeloaders, card sharps, ministers in temporary retirement, investment advisors, advertisement executives, lifestyle gurus, TV-show hosts, subsidy milkers, security personnel and skinheads who are careful not to produce anything of any use whatsoever? This, of course, speaks for, not against, a republic that tolerates and supports all varieties of luftmenschen without complaint. However, this subset of citizens also includes a number of ne'er-do-wells and no-goodniks, bellyachers and bunglers among reputable people who would earlier have been considered ordinary. There are no statistics to quantify them and no psychology to plumb the dark abysses of intelligence.

And yet, the system functions smoothly as a whole if you don't look too closely. There must be hidden resources at play, residue of voluntary efforts, imperturbable good nature and mysterious diligence that keep things running. There is no other way to explain our contentment in discontent.

Or should we look for the secret to Europe's habitability in her institutions? After all, there are still remains of democracy and the rule of law. Firemen generally come when there's a fire, the city gardeners take care of the pansies, and the district courts regularly sentence shoplifters. There is no shortage of traffic tickets or tax assessments. Nonetheless, it's fair to ask if the subterranean energy that ensures our survival is attributable to wise governance, or if the situation is rather the opposite. Does anything that flourishes here do so *despite* rather than *because* of governments that are constantly passing new regulations, decrees and

directives intended to nip any productive movement in the bud?

The Kingdom of Belgium, a small country that harbours doubts about its own existence, has proven that a country can manage quite well without a government. Starting in April 2010, a reign of *as if* lasted for over a year there. The Belgian prime minister only acted as if he were heading the nation, no one seemed bothered by the appalling state of affairs. Quite the contrary, the Belgians seemed delighted to be left in peace. The city gardeners continued to water the flowers in the Park of Laeken as if the permanent crisis in the government had nothing to do with them. Sound and unsound business practices prospered as before, tax collectors sat back and did nothing, and the famous Belgian pralines were of the finest quality, just as they've always been.

How could this be? To speak of a pervasive sense of trust would surely be excessive. Only someone with a screw loose would take at face value reports in the media or statements issued by the countless crisis summits. Every campaign promise is immediately discounted by the electorate. A bank that tried to convince its clients that it deserves their trust would reap only ridicule. No one wants to be conned.

Nevertheless, people are confident that the vegetable merchant round the corner will offer them radishes and potatoes in exchange for a colourfully printed slip of paper. Waiters and cab drivers assume their customers will pay. Those who come home late at night and flip a switch are not disconcerted when the light goes on. There are hot-dogs stands that survive without a house detective, and newspaper kiosks that manage without surveillance cameras. This disarming optimism would appear amusing if it weren't complemented by an engrained scepticism.

We are thus confronted with a puzzling combination of trust and distrust. A simple experiment could perhaps clarify this conundrum. Take a can of white paint, pour in a dash of black paint, and stir it with a stick. A pattern of exquisite complexity immediately appears, a marbling that resists mathematical explanation. Of course, you can keep stirring until you get a uniform grey tone, but that only happens when our mixture behaves like an isolated system. In reality, however, this is never the case. New ingredients always come into the mix, as if someone were constantly adding new colours to our experiment, torrents of black or white pigment. We ourselves are the reason the turbulence does not abate but increases, that the improbable always keeps the upper hand and that the unpredictable prevails.

HONOURABLE AND LESS HONOURABLE
PROFESSIONS

The habit of always drawing distinctions is a difficult one to break. And yet, it's easy to show people how tenacious their bad habits are. They have always been aware that there are different skin colours and different languages—there are said to be more than 6,000 of the latter. People are constantly focused on whether another is young or old, good-looking or unattractive, good-natured or ornery. And then there are the differences of gender, class and caste. The number of differences grows continuously and with it the kinds of possible discrimination also increase.

The United Nations, the European Commission, and their subordinate authorities work hard to defuse these with the assistance of numerous commissioners for equality. The gender mainstreaming mandate came along at just the right moment but setbacks are always to be feared.

However, there is no need to panic. There is great progress to report. Bondage has been abolished, human trafficking is banned, political pressure is being exerted on the caste system in India, the rights of the Sami people in Scandinavia have been recognized and even the Ainu and Burakumin peoples in Japan can now apparently take up whatever profession they choose and marry outside their caste.

Even stratified class societies now exist only as decoration, except in dictatorships where it survives in the form of a nomenklatura cut off from the rest of the population. In Mitteleuropa, things are different. A title of nobility is no longer required to serve in our foreign ministry and the Aryans have fortunately all disappeared.

Still, it wasn't so long ago in our part of the world that a strict separation was made between honest and dishonest people. The latter group encompassed more than criminals who were summarily flogged, quartered or broken on the wheel. In fact, a whole spectrum of professions was held to be disreputable. According to the trusty *Concise Dictionary of German Superstitions*, a 10-volume work published between 1927 and 1942, the vast array of professions that were subject to discrimination included the following: barber, barker, executioner, tinker, knacker, gravedigger, rag picker, peddler, street-sweeper, bailiff, athlete, grinder, prostitute, dream reader, wrestler, clairvoyant and snake oil salesman. The precise social status of beggars, millers, shepherds, tax collectors and usurers is not specified.

The so-called vagrants played a particularly ambiguous role. This category included entertainers and buffoons, conjurers and thimbleriggers, tightrope walkers, jugglers and acrobats, magicians, trick riders, animal tamers, too, but also musicians, dancers, minstrels and comedians. Surprisingly, the word 'gypsy' is missing from the list. Indeed, it would hardly be used today either, since these peoples now go by different names.

For contemporary readers, the list enumerated in the *Concise Dictionary* will no doubt evoke the 'dark Middle Ages', which, of course, never existed. In fact, the concept of itinerant peoples originated in pagan, oriental and ancient traditions. The Church, too, had always regarded these 'dishonest people' with suspicion, threatening them with excommunication and refusing them burial in sacred ground for centuries.

A distant echo of our list can be found in Karl Marx, who endeavoured over 1,500 pages to differentiate productive from unproductive labour. This was, as we will see, no easy task. Mistresses, musicians, equerries, clowns and jugglers appear on his list, which he expanded to include policemen, low-ranking officials, solicitors and badly paid artists.

For centuries, usurers have presented a special case that is not without interest. Their occupation was not considered honourable. Its dubious reputation was attributable to the ban on charging interest propounded in the Bible and the Quran. This ban has been upheld in the Islamic world, but as in Christendom, there has never been a shortage of tricks to circumvent it. In the twelfth century, the Pope allowed Jews to practice usury but not his faithful. This positive discrimination was immediately followed by a negative one and in the latter's wake came pogroms at first and later genocide.

Nevertheless, the Catholic Church did rescind its restrictions against these 'financial service providers', albeit with a significant delay, to wit, in the nineteenth century.

Isn't it wonderful how times have changed? There can no longer be any talk of discrimination against most of the professions that were once considered dishonest. On the contrary! Those who have followed these callings not only enjoy an upright, well-earned position but are also at the top of the social ladder as far as reputation and earnings are concerned.

In the twentieth century, the barkers of yore have risen to become heads of prominent advertising agencies, buffoons have mutated into entertainers, anchormen and emcees. Even the modest barbers have become plastic surgeons and the carnival clairvoyants have moulted into highly compensated chief economists. Beauty queens and supermodels have left the red-light district far behind. The descendants of the card sharps are well-respected investment advisers. The most magnificent career was allotted to gladiators, escape artists and other carnival performers. Anyone turning his nose up at athletes today will suffer the same scorn to which they had been subjected in old days. Sports figures, above all, the great soccer players, are the icons of our globalized world. No butcher can hope to earn anywhere near as much as they do, nor can any politician dream of being as popular.

Stars, once at home in Hollywood where they were invented, can now be found in almost every field— celebrity chefs, dentists, architects, lawyers and coiffeurs.

However, they are forced to live with an ugly 'VIP' brand on their foreheads and are usually surrounded by a train of photographers, fans and bodyguards when they don't have spokespersons to represent them for the sake of simplicity. A horde of agents, impresarios, managers and producers fills this function, thereby strongly contributing to the economic performance of this particular line of business.

In this triumphal parade of once-vilified professions, it is those previously known as usurers who break ranks—as they have often done over the course of history. The magnates of finance have amassed more wealth, power and influence than ever before, but their social standing has lately been dealt a significant blow in the wake of recent crises. They may now take some comfort in the saying, 'Once your reputation is gone, you've got nothing left to lose.'

It's another matter entirely for artists, who have been lumped together with itinerant peoples, with less than honourable folks, or in a later term, with bohemians, for as long as our collective memory extends. For a time, they made a virtue of this necessity and proudly behaved like outsiders. Today, millions of people dream of belonging to this admired host. Entire generations recall the world tours of pop and rock bands as the highlights of their existence. Every season a continent hangs on the lips of competing pop singers. Music festivals proliferate across the country, 'cultural capitals' blossom in the most remote provinces. Prices at auctions for 'installations' and 'works in progress' of contemporary art far overshadow those of works by Goya and Caspar David Friedrich. High- and lowbrow have buried the hatchet. Bayreuth and Salzburg music festivals compete for prime-time slots with the live folk-music TV show *Musikantenstadl*. Who could see this cultural pandemonium and not feel satisfied?

Even villains cannot escape rehabilitation. Convicted serial killers write bestsellers and hawk the rights to the movie industry. Marx, who had no lack of compendia, foresaw it all when others were still trying to distinguish between honest and dishonest professions.

> A philosopher produces ideas, a poet poems, a clergyman sermons, a professor compendia and so on. A criminal produces crimes. If we take a closer look at the connection between this latter branch of production and society as a whole, we shall rid ourselves of many prejudices . . . The criminal produces the police and the criminal justice system, constables, judges, executioners, juries, etc.; and all these develop different capacities of the human mind, create new needs, and new ways of satisfying them. Torture alone has given rise to the most ingenious mechanical inventions and employed many honourable craftsmen in the production of its instruments . . . The criminal [. . . also produces] art, belles-lettres, novels, and even tragedies . . . The criminal breaks the monotony and everyday security of bourgeois life. In this way he keeps it from stagnation . . . Would locks

ever have reached their present degree of excellence had there been no thieves? Would the making of bank notes have reached its present perfection had there been no forgers? . . . And if one leaves the sphere of private crime: would the world-market ever have come into being but for national crime?

WHY EVERYTHING ALWAYS LEAVES SPOTS

*It rained so hard that all the pigs got clean
and all the people dirty.*

G. C. Lichtenberg

Have you noticed that it's almost impossible to drink a cup of coffee without leaving a smudge, a trickle, a spatter, a spot, a puddle or a stain on the cup's rim, the saucer, your napkin, the teaspoon, your shirt or your blouse? Roughly 95 per cent of the time, coffee pot designers have been unable to create a pot that can pour the aromatic liquid in a smooth stream without leaving any visible traces. Variously shaped spouts have had as little effect on this result as the expedient favoured by our grandmothers. They would stretch a rubber band between a hook and a small cylinder of foam rubber: the drop catcher.

Why have philosophers disregarded the problem of spotting? Even Heraclitus spared little thought to his shirt when he came to the conclusion that everything flows. The reason is simple: for the most part they left the battle against dirt to others. The spill must be wiped up immediately, the saucer rinsed, the shirt laundered.

But by whom? I'll give you three guesses. It wasn't the philosophers who had to worry about grime, but women. For the most part maids, housekeepers and washerwomen took on this task. And yet, as the *Odyssey* shows, even the daughters of kings, like the beautiful Nausicaa, along with her handmaidens, had to work on washday:

> Now when they came to the beautiful streams of the river, where were the washing tanks that never failed—for abundant clear water welled up from beneath and flowed over, to cleanse garments however soiled—there they loosed the mules from under the wagon and drove them along the eddying river to graze on the honey-sweet water-grass, and themselves took in their arms the raiment from the wagon, and bore it into the dark water, and trampled it in the trenches, busily vying each with each. Now when they had washed the garments, and had cleansed them of all the stains, they spread them out in rows on the shore of the sea where the waves dashing against the land washed the pebbles cleanest.

Over the centuries, the exertions required to do battle against dirt have been heroic and the quantity of energy and material it has consumed is immeasurable. Even those who don't trust statistics will be alarmed to hear that more than 620,000 tonnes of detergent is used each year in Germany. Worldwide consumption is reputed to

exceed 22 million tonnes. 'Washing will always be necessary,' a leading industry executive explains. He is right,
just like the German saying attributed to a street-sweeper,
'Dirt is my bread and butter.'

The number of soaps, powders, pellets, sprays and
liquids deployed in cleaning laundry is abundant. The
array of stain removers is possibly even greater. If you
type it into a search engine, you will be able to gape at
25,000 brightly coloured illustrations. If you find this
excess intimidating, you can restrict your search to dry
cleaners. Initially, practitioners went into combat with
dirt using turpentine, benzol and petroleum naphtha,
but they soon realized they needed newer and more
powerful substances for the front lines.

It wasn't long before it became clear that every
attempt to get rid of dirt threatened to draw them into
a vicious circle as the cleaning material itself became a
new source of pollution. Niklas Luhmann formulated
a classical description of this dilemma: 'The brush that
brushes a brush always leaves behind a few bristles.'

No one using it can know exactly what is in a spoon-
ful of detergent. Those who would like to inform themselves can turn to the six-volume *Handbook of Detergents*.
Apparently, it contains dozens of surfactants with
unpronounceable names in addition to builders, stabi-
lizers, optical brighteners and synthetic perfumes. The
dangers these substances pose are considerable and
again and again new regulations were necessary counter
them. As a rule, the once-celebrated hydrogen chlorides

like trichloroethylene and methyl chloroform were restricted from most applications because they were proven flammable, harmful to the environment and to health, or carcinogenic. (Only perchloroethylene is still tolerated, albeit reluctantly.) And who would be willing to swear that special esters, silane or aliphatic compounds are an efficient corrective?

The attempt to remove all stains is fraught with difficulties and as laudable as it is to concern oneself with sanitary conditions, that too has peculiar side effects. New studies have shown that parents who persevere in protecting their children from dangerous germs often achieve the opposite—they end up weakening their offspring's immune system. One could make a case that too little dirt is unhealthy.

Distressed nurturers can find reassurance in the fact that a completely sterile environment need not be feared. Anyone involved with a high-tech industrial facility and biological laboratories can tell you a thing or two about how difficult it is to create a germ-free environment. One cubic metre of 'fresh air' has on average 35,000,000 particles larger than a half micron. Who can guarantee that there aren't a few micro-organisms among them? It's impossible to eliminate them completely. Having no more than 12 particles per cubic metre floating around in a clean room of the highest quality is a happy result.

There is no other way to put it—even the void has something in it. Like absolute zero, a perfect vacuum is unattainable. Only approximations are possible, measured on a scale that stretches from coarse through high to ultra high. A scanning tunnelling microscope and particle accelerators are required to reach the highest levels. But even someone able to achieve a pressure of $10-12$ millibar has to count on a swarm of 10,000 molecules per cubic centimetre. Conditions in interstellar and intergalactic space are more propitious than on Earth, but even there, at least one particle can be found in each cubic centimetre. In other words: the ideal state in Buddhism, nirvana, is apparently only possible in the other world.

These simple reflections lead inevitably to one conclusion—purity does not exist in nature. No matter what scale of measurement you use, from astrophysics to subatomic particles, the world reveals itself to be tremendously promiscuous. Admixture, contamination, confusion, hotchpotch, cohabitation, transformation, mishmash is the norm. Those who find this formulation to be too common can employ the more sophisticated concept of entropy. It is, in fact, impurity that enables the body's most crucial functions like nutrition, respiration and reproduction.

The foregoing makes crystal clear that striving for cleanliness is a futile, pointless and endless effort that only we are fixated on. Human beings are the only species interested in cleanliness. (Cat lovers will contest this, presenting their loved ones' careful grooming as evidence. However, as simple counterevidence: no cat ever came up with the idea of vacuuming, washing windows and regularly disinfecting its toilet.) What explains this peculiar behaviour of *Homo sapiens*? It's difficult for anyone who is a member of the species to answer. But what if we changed perspectives? People assume that they are the ones who cause the stains. They believe that they're dirtying their environment which they presume is clean. Yet they are mistaken. For what we see as staining does not come from us. Our surroundings are filled with spots and spillage and yet we are the only ones who decide what is dirty and what is not. The universe knows no such categories, nor does it care about them.

An extreme case may clarify the matter. The American aviator, business tycoon and filmmaker Howard Hughes feared the outside world his entire life. He was unable to leave the room in which he lived for months at a time. Before he dared touch an object, he wrapped his hand in a fresh paper towel that was then destroyed by a staff member. Everywhere he looked, this poor man saw threatening spots and spatters, dust motes and bacteria. It is said that he died, non compos mentis, of malnutrition.

Medical textbooks give the diagnosis of obsessive-compulsive disorder for this condition, specifically ablutomania. One can hardly deny that this symptom, at least in a milder form, is part of man's basic configuration. Perhaps the obsessive inclination to wash ourselves and our surroundings is even part of our genetic makeup.

There is no objective guide to which substances should be removed in any given situation, rather the decision is influenced by a number of subjective conditions that offer no common denominator. A treatise on dirt would be necessary to bring some clarity to the question. I will, unfortunately, have to settle for a few suggestions. It's interesting that some substances which are considered clean become dirty as soon as they are in the wrong place. For example, butter is above suspicion but becomes disturbing as a grease spot on a condolence letter or an engraving by Albrecht Dürer. The same man who prefers a very rare steak to one well done starts to panic when he cuts his finger or suffers a bloody nose. Signs of virility are deeply admired in some circumstances whereas in others there is a marked preference for a virgin birth.

With organic and inorganic substances, we draw a strict distinction between those that soil and those that do not. Shit doubtless plays a central role among the former. Other excreta can change in the blink of an eye from signs of vigour to filth. Christian Enzensberger, who has immersed himself more deeply in this question than most, has determined that 'human beings excrete twenty-five substances', a number that must be hard to top.

Not only does the source of the smudge matter but also its contents and consistency. Is it sticky, oily, greasy or slimy or is it dry? In the latter case, it would most likely be considered dust and disliked. Lichtenberg had it right: 'The elegant dance of motes in a ray of sunlight is nothing more than whirling dirt.' Nevertheless, it is to their credit that flakes, fuzz and dander simply fall without leaving a stain. Dust is attacked with cloths, brushes, brooms and vacuum cleaners, not with scrubbers, mops and pails. It's a Sisyphean labour that at best temporarily displaces the dust. The sedate, dry character of all that crumbles and collapses instead of dampening seems pleasant and touching. In response to indiscreet questions, Germans will retort *Das geht dich einen feuchten Dreck an*, or *It's none of your damp dirt*. Only when dampness is involved does staining turn dramatic. The scandalous urgency inherent in smudging evokes embarrassment, anger and schadenfreude not only in silent movies. Eggs, tomatoes or cream pies are thrown in protest to exploit the horror felt by the targets of these staining missiles.

This is all annoying but relatively harmless. Things only become serious when morality is brought to bear on the compulsion to clean. For the Puritans, as their name suggests, no human society could be pure enough. Their suspicion that as soon as something is 'greased', corruption, the mafia and blackmail are soon to follow is well founded. Even the whitest waistcoat is soon spotted. As soon as one's sense of honour is besmirched, all hell breaks loose because those stains can't be removed with simple spot remover. Whether the injured resort to a duel, an honour killing or a blood feud is simply a question of style. Yet when purity laws transcend the private sphere and become a collective obsession, the results are even more disastrous. The compulsion for cleanliness, transmuted into ideological or ethnic fixations, leads to mass murder.

In contrast, the private use of soap or detergent, however bizarre a form it may take, seems comforting. Nevertheless, the nagging question of why everything stains has never been adequately answered. The only comfort for those who ask is the thought of the victory of the human spirit over spots and stains of all kinds in the last 200 years. In honour of the many unknown inventors to whom we owe washing machines and dishwashers, let me name but a few: Jacob Christian Schäffer of Regensburg, Nathaniel Briggs of New Hampshire, Josephine Cochrane and Alva J. Fisher of Illinois. Let us celebrate their memory! And long live . . .

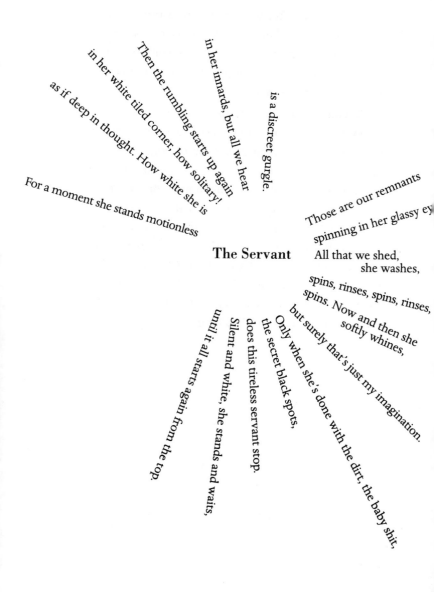

The Servant

in her innards, but all we hear

is a discreet gurgle.

Then the rumbling starts up again

in her white tiled corner, how solitary!

as if deep in thought. How white she is

For a moment she stands motionless

Those are our remnants
spinning in her glassy ey[e]

All that we shed,
she washes,

spins, rinses, spins, rinses,
spins. Now and then she
softly whines,

but surely that's just my imagination.

Only when she's done with the dirt, the baby shit,
the secret black spots,
does this tireless servant stop.

Silent and white, she stands and waits,

until it all starts again from the top.

IT'S A GIFT!

Thou shalt not muzzle the ox
when he treadeth out the corn
Deuteronomy 25:4

In a society steeped in social democracy like the Federal Republic of Germany, privileges do not get good press. The mantra of social justice sees to that. The principle of equality, long cherished by the Left, survives in diluted form and yet maintains its symbolic hegemony. Thus every prerogative, whether of an individual or a group, is politically highly suspect. In these circumstances the charge of *feudalism* is often raised, and references to social class are always popular. Less frequent are reminders that modern dictatorships granted their supporters privileges with far less restraint than any absolute monarchy. The Soviet nomenklatura were shameless in this respect. Former GDR officials were egregious enough to call the brand of fashionable clothing available to the general public outside the standard stores at obscenely high prices the 'Exquisite' line.

Naturally the same privileges that are condemned in theory are highly sought after in practice and, once obtained, they are defended tooth and nail. This rule applies as much in North Korea as in the United States. It blooms most spectacularly, however, only where the market rules. When demand is high, there can be no lack of offers. That's why there is a profusion of products touted as exclusive in every shopping centre. This attribute adorns not only luxury yachts and day spas but stockings and toilet paper to boot. Clients are meant to feel that they are part of a small, particularly select minority, for Tom, Dick and Harry have no way of acquiring these goods—a form of discrimination that not a single commissioner for equality has yet denounced.

Through a wealth of bonus awards, discounts, special offers and loyalty programmes, regular consumers are encouraged to become premium clients. Airlines use finely calibrated system of gradation to ensure that some passengers will travel hunched and contorted in their seats while others will stretch out in freshly made beds. The class struggle has been privatized in many ways and waged with the help of silver, gold, platinum, even diamond-studded credit cards. These are meant to impress upon the people that the privileged have never been more privileged than they are today.

The opposition of being and seeming is often interpreted in moral terms as an indication of the unavoidable and now general hypocrisy necessary for a more or less peaceful coexistence to be at all possible in a society. This interpretation assumes that the hypocrite is unaware of his hypocrisy because it has become a matter of course for him. However fitting this may be, the self-righteous undertone is grating. Rather than morality—which only goes so far—it would perhaps be more constructive to look at economic systems that predate the monetary economy. Long before coins and banknotes, interest and credit were invented, there were gifts; the creation of privilege came later. What both have in common is that they cannot be demanded, only granted.

In a manifesto from the 1848, we read that capitalism has left 'no other bond between man and man than naked self-interest, than callous "cash payment".' A strong statement, but is it true? Millennia-old customs, deeply rooted in the psyche, can be suppressed, discouraged and manipulated but they never entirely disappear. That is why superstition survives quite happily inside us. The Enlightenment was not able to do away with magical thinking and animism. Since Neolithic civilization left behind no documents, we must rely on assumptions and ethnographic finds to approach it. This is particularly true of the oldest strata of the human economy. We know that gifts predate goods. In ancient societies the giving of gifts was regulated by a complex, highly ritualized set of rules. Rank, prestige and social status were not decided by the accumulation of wealth but by the way it was distributed. Traces of this attitude persist, and not just in Japan, where gifts must be meticulously prepared, wrapped and offered on particular occasions with established ceremoniousness. This distinguishes the gifts from any commercial transaction.

The same applies to privileges that cannot be negotiated but only bestowed. Evidence of this can be found in every family. The easy-going, incorrigible bon vivant gets away with things his respectable brother wouldn't dream of doing. The devout niece bends over backwards for the tyrannical old grandmother. The pleasant nephew is offered money that will leave a hole in the budget by the end of the month. The Indian construction worker engages himself in the United Arab Emirates for slave wages so that his son will have money to pay a dowry. All of this transcends any 'callous cash payment'.

Ancient customs have not disappeared from the normal workplace either. Every land registry lists all sorts of easements and old hunting, fishing, timber, water and access rights. There must still be places where the pastor is given a whole goose on a specific day of the year. In traditional professions like mining, the venerable custom of wages in kind persists. Long before wage settlements, each miner received a certain amount of coal for his own use. Brewers, distillers and vintners similarly received a portion of the 'house drink'. Railway employees enjoy free travel; airhostesses fly for free on their holidays; literary critics receive as many reading copies as they can possibly desire. In respectable bakeries, apprentice bakers don't have to pay for their lunchtime roll. Refusing them bread is considered tantamount to taking food from their mouths.

Such laxness is like a pebble in the shoe of justice and sand in the gears of bureaucracy. Germans may remember the 'Maultaschen case' of 2009 in which a 58-year-old geriatric nurse was summarily fired from her job in a nursing home where she had been employed for 17 years for taking home six leftover Maultaschen, a type of large stuffed pasta. The local court found the sentence fitting.

In earlier days, before smoking was considered a public health hazard, workers in cigar and cigarette factories were allowed a ration of the said poison to take home. Today the nicotine privilege is granted only to retired Chancellor Helmut Kohl, who has resisted all forms of re-education. Diplomatic passports also spare their holders much unpleasantness, just as certain plastic identification cards allow their bearers to jump queues. For public servants, a number of benefits are common, including performance or responsibility bonuses, rent subsidies and cost of living allowances. Politicians can scarcely avoid expense allowances or pension commitments, and the private sector teems with exorbitant bonuses and severance packages. It goes without saying that these special rights and privileges are kept under wraps as far as possible so as not to attract envy.

One's profession alone does not determine preferential treatment that violates the fundamental principle of equality. Those who hold the Bavarian Order of Merit can ride for free, whenever the spirit moves them, on the Starnberg ferry or on the steamboats *Herrsching* and *Diesen*. Oh those orders of merit with their carefully calibrated ranks, grades and classes from simple medals to the Grand Cross star special class with its sash and eight-pointed star! Anyone who feels slighted in this area cannot level charges of discrimination in any administrative court. Even if he were willing to offer a callous cash payment, he would get no joy from the Office of the Federal President. The Order runs on favour and grace, anachronisms from monarchical times. Prisoners condemned in a court of law are also at the mercy of such benevolence and grace, should they hope to have their sentences commuted. Man's desire to donate and endow can no more be eradicated than his longing for privileges and the small gifts that are understood as testaments of friendship. In my country alone, it is estimated that every year foundations receive between 2 and 5 billion euros, even though no one can calculate the philanthropic or charitable effect of these institutions, whose promotion and administrative costs can run up to 40 per cent of the budget.

Not everyone condones such sweeping largesse. The more money wealthy men like the billionaires Bill Gates and Warren Buffett give away, the more suspiciously they are regarded. They are reproached for wanting only to soothe their conscience, reduce their tax bill or put on a good front. Their philanthropy is nothing more than a new way of buying indulgences. Leftist ideologues worry that donations of that kind undermine the class struggle; market radicals caution against coddling the needy; trade unions see their claim to sole representation threatened as soon as anyone tries to act on their own accord without sitting down at the joint negotiating table. These objections seem more than a little petty and narrow-minded.

In contrast, small retailers, mercurial as their business is, have always known how to make hay from this proclivity for gifts and giving. A butcher will gladly offer a small child a bit of sausage. Perfume counters are filled with free samples. People are used to honouring customs much older than double-entry bookkeeping. Every opportunity can be made to serve the bottom line, even the flimsiest pretexts like Mother's Day or Valentine's Day. Weddings and birthdays are even better. Even the births themselves must be celebrated according to long-standing traditions, especially when, as on Christmas, the point is to welcome a new god.

But who has the hardest time coming to terms with gifts? The state, of course. It is displeased when its citizen evade its control and offer or receive a gift without asking permission. Whenever gifts are exchanged, the treasury bares its teeth. The clearest evidence of this is the gift tax which penalizes generosity. The tax office keeps a particularly close eye on company Christmas parties. Any gift worth more than 10 euros must be registered in an account kept by the giver which records who received what, because the recipient must report taxes on values exceeding that amount. This follows the doctrine of 'equalizing monetary advantages' any gift might bring to the recipient. Article 37b of the German revenue tax code is intended, with absurd thoroughness and rat-like greed, to keep all such gifts to an absolute minimum.

There is but one exception to these sanctions and that applies, of course, to the sitting government which lavishes tax gifts whenever an election approaches. This obscene concept conveys nothing more than that the state considers everything it takes from its citizens as its lawful property which it can dispose of as it wishes. When it does give something back, it expects gratitude to be deposited in the voting urns.

The German philosopher Peter Sloterdijk caused a scandal a few years ago when he made a case for 'The Revolution of the Giving Hand'. He asked if it wouldn't be better to replace the compulsory payment of taxes with voluntary contributions by the citizens. He could have invoked the influential anthropologist Marcel Mauss, who wrote, 'We should come out of ourselves and regard the duty of giving as a liberty, for in it there lies no risk.' A fine Maori proverb runs: *Ko maru kai atu / Ko maru kai mai / Ka ngohe ngohe*—give as much as you receive and all will be for the best.' Another anthropologist, Pierre Clastres, who studied indigenous cultures of South America, came to the conclusion: 'Greed and power are incompatible; to be a chief it is necessary to be generous.' That, of course, was a long time ago and should not be confused with Rousseau's idyllic fantasy of noble savages, uncorrupted by civilization.

Sloterdijk's courage is admirable as is the naivety with which he waded into the minefield of voluntariness. This did not prevent his adversaries from attacking him with as much fury and malice as if he had desecrated one of the nation's most sacred cows. In fact, he not only played the gift economy against business economics but also violated the principle of equality by speaking of the exploitation of the productive by the unproductive.

On this question, the Gini coefficient, a measure of statistical dispersion that quantifies inequality of income, instructs us that equality is a fiction, because in most countries, including our own, wealth and income are distributed very unevenly. In recent decades, these disparities have only increased. Put differently, ever-more privileges are bestowed on ever-fewer people. One reason for this is that the wealthy in our age, unlike in the times of clans and class divisions, no longer distribute favours and privileges to others but serve themselves first and foremost.

This self-empowerment can have only one effect— it makes the wish to abolish all privilege overpowering. But that would be a shame. Experience teaches us that all we can expect is the bare minimum being meted out to all, in which case everyone's portion is one and the same. An opposite tack is more compelling: grant privileges to everyone but in such a way that each person receives something different than anyone else on the simple grounds that no two people are alike. This demand may seem audacious but it is more humane than most of the utopian ideas we know from history.

IS SCIENCE A SECULAR RELIGION?

It depends. Like religion, science has a propensity for the plural, for example, hard sciences, applied sciences, auxiliary sciences or cutting-edge sciences. Which one now wears the crown? Wasn't it once philosophy or, a few centuries later, theology? Mathematics has always enjoyed a certain esteem. Today, at any rate, it's the natural sciences that call the tune. They pride themselves on their precision and rigour. Leaders in the field revere the distinction between hard and soft sciences, although they are polite enough not to dismiss the liberal arts, social and cultural sciences, in public as an elevated form of drivel. Economic valuations offer a more tangible judgement. The 'soft' sciences have long been the poor cousins. They can only dream of the billion-dollar budgets that physicists, biologists and astronomers have at their disposal. Their financial resources are too paltry for them to step on religion's turf either.

The outlook is different for the natural scientists. They go whole hog. This leads not only to conflict but also to institutional similarities. Like the great churches, natural scientists dispose of their own more or less extraterritorial domains. The secular universities, academies, institutes and laboratories are the scientists' equivalent of temple precincts, cathedrals and cloisters. Remains of pomp and ritual survive in the form of columned rooms, gowns and ceremonial garb in universities from Harvard to Heidelberg. It is not by chance that the validation of a student's qualifications is called 'academic consecration'. Researchers, like priests, have a fondness for jargon impenetrable to lay persons. Ecclesiastical Latin and Church Slavonic, like Quranic Arabic, are far removed from colloquial speech. The former remind one of the peculiar English with which scientists from all over the world communicate. Only a few initiates will profit from works like *Structure and Properties of 1,2-Dithiolylium-4-methide, 1,2-Dithiolylium-4-olate and 1,2-Dithiolylium-4-thiolate: A MO Study at the HF- and Post-HF Level*, or take note of *The Large N Limit of Superconformal Field Theories and Supergravity*. This is no reflection on their relevance.

Like religions, the sciences are also hierarchically organized. The hierarchical ladder from deacon and priest to bishop and cardinal correspond to the academic degrees from baccalaureate to masters and from doctorate to institute director. The only thing scientists are missing is a Holy See. When someone is referred to as a 'pope of science', there's no mistaking the sardonic undertone. To this extent, Protestantism has conquered the scientific world, although Catholic practices like beatification and canonization are not entirely unfamiliar. The Nobel Prize is a kind of canonization.

There are other points of resemblance between the rules, written and unwritten, of both systems. Falsification and plagiarism are punished like blasphemy and sacrilege. In such cases, peer reviews and expert reports function like canon law, synods or the Commission on Faith and Order. However, it is less clear how disputes are to be settled. Who decides to whom priority should be accorded? Where are ecumenical borders to be drawn? These questions trouble both camps. There is much to be said about the similarities and differences in interaction, in official attire, financing and informal customs. But these are details best left to ethnologists.

On the other hand, there is one similarity that is of particular interest—the comprehensive claim to the truth both religions and the 'exact' sciences advance. This renders adherents of both camps extremely sensitive to outside attacks. The conflicts this sensitivity gave rise to throughout history are legendary and still echo in the present day. Stories of overlapping and reciprocal interests between the scientific and religious worlds garner much less attention. Some are reluctant to admit that, in the Middle Ages, the clergy ensured the continuation of scholarship. Our philosophical inheritance from the ancient world was brought to Europe by Islamic theologians and survived primarily in the monasteries. The polymath Albertus Magnus, who was interested in botany, zoology and mineralogy, among many other subjects, was a Dominican friar and Catholic bishop. The great logician, William of Ockham was a Franciscan monk. Nicolaus Copernicus was a canon in Warmia.

Johannes Kepler was a student in a monastery before becoming an evangelical theologian.

The intellectual border crossing between religion and science did not end with the Middle Ages: Isaac Newton spent decades studying theology, mysticism and alchemy; Leonhard Euler defended the Bible against the Freethinkers; the foundational discoveries of genetics were made by the Augustinian monk Gregor Mendel; Georg Cantor, the inventor of set theory, believed the theory of transfinite numbers had been communicated to him by God; Max Planck was deeply religious and always took his position as churchwarden seriously; and Kurt Gödel, the great mathematical logician of the Modern era, devoted the end of his life to formulating a proof of God's existence.

The irreconcilability of religion and science is hardly a given. Scholars have pursued the most heated controversies in their own domains, not against the opposition. For Christians it was about the Trinity, the Eucharist or predestination. In Islam, it concerned the Prophet's succession. The battle between two doctrines or two fatwas could have murderous consequences. Theological differences have often escalated to bloody religious wars. Scientists must be given credit for the fact that they have rarely killed each other, certainly less often than believers have. Their battles usually take place on paper and the religious powers tolerated them within reason. The last scientist the Church burnt at the stake was Giordano Bruno. Later scientists, like Galileo, lost their sponsors in the worst-case scenario, their work was placed on the Index and they were harassed by their colleagues.

At the same time, there were always outsiders and troublemakers on both sides who became the source of their institutions' vitality and development, if not progress. Orthodoxy is lost without its heretics. This is true for churches as it is for the sciences. These epochal breaks such heretics have brought about can also be called 'paradigm shifts' as Thomas Kühn did in his influential study *The Structure of Scientific Revolutions*.

The older the institution, the harder it is to break with its dogma. The natural sciences thus have an advantage in this respect. Religions cannot keep up with their pace of innovation because their evolution has been proceeded 'more naturally', that is, more slowly.

The philosophy of the Enlightenment, however, was in a hurry. La Mettrie, Holbach and Helvétius wanted to make a clean sweep of 'the imposture of the clergy' and 'superstition'. Diderot suggested using the last priest's entrails to strangle the king and Voltaire exclaimed *'Écrasez l'infâme!'* This only became serious once the French Revolution stormed the heights of the political chain of command. With the stroke of a pen, the National Convention outlawed Catholic masses in Paris churches in 1793; cathedrals were plundered and filled with carnivalesque parades. The Jacobins wanted to replace Christianity with a cult of reason, to which they dedicated many secularized churches. They celebrated a 'Festival of Liberty' in the cathedral of Notre Dame, for which a beautiful French woman represented the Goddess of Reason. This did not please Robespierre. He proposed inventing a nebulous 'Supreme Being', who would be worshiped in numerous temples. The Hébertists and Montagnards, the atheists and deists immediately started arguing about pure doctrine. They did not have enough time for a religious war; after 10 years, the attempt to do away with an old religion by decree and set a new one up overnight had foundered.

Later atheists pinned their hopes on the quiet, peaceful work of secularization and assumed that churches would gradually be emptied out on their own. By the turn of the twentieth century, they had to realize they'd been mistaken. Sects in North America, like Islam, showed signs of unexpected vitality. The world learnt once again to differentiate dozens of denominations. Sunnis and Shiites, Wahabis, Isma'ilis, Zaydis and Alawites were making headlines just like the Anabaptists, evangelicals and born-again Christians. Schisms yawned open on all sides. New Age followers, scientologists and obscure revivalist preachers captured the market. Hateful superstition, from astrology to esotericism raised its head anew. New forms of militancy gained political influence in Tehran as well as in the White House.

The high priests of Reason were surely filled with disgust and bitterness when they suddenly found themselves on the defensive again. Old clashes were reignited. Scientists and philosophers like Richard Dawkins, Sam Harris, Stephen Hawking and Michael Onfray took over the bestseller lists with books like *The God Delusion*, *The*

End of Faith and *Atheist Manifesto*. The notorious gadfly Christopher Hitchens joined the fray, declaring, 'God is not great!'

American neuroscientists reported, as La Mettrie once did, that 'we are just machines'. This was not very original. Evangelists of artificial intelligence can hardly be satisfied with such reprises. Like Ray Kurzweil, a tech-guru from MIT, they want to save humanity from itself. Kurzweil hopes that in 15 years it will be possible for us to reprogram our biology using biotechnology, which in turn will enable us to live long enough for nanotechnology to develop the means to let us live for ever. Until then, the prophet knows how to make do. 'To slow the ageing process, you take 250 dietary supplements a day?'—'I'm down to 200 because of greater efficiency.' Kurzweil was inducted into the National Inventors Hall of Fame more than a decade ago. The man is well connected. Larry Page, a founder of Google, is one of his admirers. Apple and NASA support Kurzweil as well. No wonder he's in a good mood. Yet the fervent tone in which he spins his fantasy of omnipotence is strange. As is often the case the proclaimer of a new 'Weltan-schauung' has been contaminated by his adversaries and adopts their attitude of infallibility without being aware of it. And so he becomes a missionary and atheism a religion.

Fortunately, those who put complete faith in science are only a minority of all scientists. Just as a cardinal can afford the luxury of doubt more easily than the pious maiden aunt in the confessional, the cleverest scientists often greet questions about their certainties with a confident smile. Yet they keep an ironic distance from religion. Einstein once wrote, 'For me the Jewish religion like all others is an incarnation of the most childish superstitions.' With the same chutzpah he concluded, 'Science without religion is lame, religion without science is blind.'

In any case, the faction of doctrinaires, zealots and fanatics who are unable to bear the unfathomable is less significant than the noise they make. There is no need to fear them because, as the fearless Paul Feyerabend put it, those who spread the most fear are merely mice in ill-fitting lion's clothing. Their reconstruction of the eighteenth-century disputes is barren and unproductive even if cloaked in the most advanced technology. Do they really have nothing better to do than to waste their time and ours with unanswerable questions? Couldn't they spare the world their foolish attempts to replace religion with science and science with religion?

ALEXANDER VON HUMBOLDT
AND THE BATTLE BETWEEN INTELLIGENCE
AND POWER

We have, in Germany, a beloved if shop-soiled role-playing game, in which two parties formerly known as 'Intelligence' and 'Power' are matched up in all sorts of exhibition fights. According to this ritual, the political class of eggheads, also known as Intellectuals, are considered irksome troublemakers and most of those who belong to the guild of scribblers behave like they are the upholders of freedom of speech, progress, human rights and all other such fine things. In times of censorship, the wrestling match between 'mind' and 'might' is far from even but, in the end, the writers mostly have more staying power. The ministers they heckled have faded into oblivion whereas their banned books are still on the shelves.

One would think, given present conditions, at least in our republic, that this spectacle has had its day. Only the older veterans remember with emotion the bouts of mutual insults so common in the era of the late Franz Josef Strauss, long-time CSU chairman and minister-president of Bavaria. Since then, these opponents have developed a symbiotic relationship evident on every TV channel. Politicians and intellectuals now appear to be dependent on each other, not just in endless talk shows but also in the consulting business, in policy decisions, commissions and hearings, whether the matter at hand is climate or energy, education, assisted suicide or the euro.

It almost seems like our country has adopted a civilized tone. All for the best? The end of animosity? Perhaps this harmless impression is deceptive. Not only because a whiff of opportunism hangs over their palaver, which usually remains without consequence, but also because division of labour between the two clans is as precarious as it ever was. This is reason enough to recall the traps our forefathers in the nineteenth century would set for each other.

A renowned German intellectual, who died in Berlin almost 160 years ago, is a perfect example of such ritualized duelling. Alexander von Humboldt was a master of this German specialty. He honed tactical and strategic skills that are worth studying. In his skirmishes with power, Humboldt had more resources at his disposal than most of his contemporaries. They, for the most part, were poor devils constrained to engage themselves as tutors, librarians or hack writers in tiny principalities. Humboldt's family belonged to the service gentry and gave him a first-rate education, an excellent network and a considerable inheritance.

These privileges, however, were offset by handicaps that did not bode well for a political career. First and foremost, there were his convictions which, contrary to the customs of his class, he absolutely refused to compromise on. Not only would he have nothing to do with established religion, his overt republicanism made him an outsider. He was also a sworn enemy of the nascent nationalism of his time. Furthermore, he insisted on complete independence of thought and action. This world citizen passed up all offers of positions as ambassador or minister, preferring instead to devote his life to scientific research.

Three examples will illustrate his strategy. It was widely known that Humboldt was obsessed with the idea of making an expedition to Latin America. At the time this continent was still a vast *terra incognita* for science. The Spanish rulers had much to hide. Not only did they forbid trade between their colonies, all foreigners were considered potential spies and therefore not allowed entry. Humboldt did not let these obstacles discourage him. He quickly learnt to speak Spanish and put his connections to work. Through a complicated manoeuvre involving a protégé of the prime minister and the prime minister's lover Queen Maria Luise, Humboldt was granted an audience at court in Aranjuez. There he successfully presented his plan to Charles IV and was given a special passport which accorded him complete freedom of action. He was not above leveraging the gossip and intrigues of the Spanish court to his own ends. Without his finely honed diplomatic skills, Humboldt would never have got his expedition off the ground.

When he returned to Europe from his grand voyage in 1804, Prussia was on the brink of defeat. What did Humboldt do? He set off for Paris at the first opportunity and spent the next 20 years there. He had good reason to—the French capital was the leading centre of scientific learning. His voluntary emigration was politically risky and earned him accusations of collaborating with the archenemy and being 'insufficiently German'. Incidentally, both the high echelon Prussian functionaries and the French autocrat found Humboldt's decision suspicious. Napoleon put him under the surveillance of his secret police and toyed with the idea of having him deported. The emperor believed he was a Prussian agent and had trouble tolerating the degree of fame Humboldt enjoyed. To protect himself from attacks, Humboldt relied not only on his friendships in political and scientific circles but also on public opinion. He realized early on that a new medium then gaining power— the international press—could offer him a modicum of protection.

His main objective in Paris was to finish his monumental work, *Voyage aux régions équinoxiales du Nouveau Continent* (Travels to the Equinoctial Regions of America). This resulting work is a magnificent, richly illustrated edition in 30 volumes, tellingly written not in German but in French and Latin. The author upped his ante by staking his personal fortune—apparently an amount

that today would be in the multimillions—to finance the project.

For several reasons, not the least of which was the exhaustion of his fortune, Humboldt was obliged to obey the Prussian king's call in 1827 to serve as court chamberlain. He reluctantly returned to Berlin. He had a lifelong aversion to this 'small, unlettered, intellectually barren and, furthermore, exceptionally malicious city' (according to Alfred Wilhelm Dove), especially since its 'prevailing atmosphere of constriction and pretention, of gaucherie and intolerance must have evoked nostalgic memories in the old lion of the Faubourg St Germain.' His position there was precarious. The chauvinists considered him cosmopolitan, the reactionaries saw him as a closet Jacobin, the anti-Semites held him to be a friend of the Jews and the bigots believed him an atheist. His adversaries' distrust was well founded. After the failed revolution of 1848, at almost 80 years of age, he followed the funeral cortège of the victims of the March Revolution with his head uncovered. For decades, his fellow courtiers did everything they could to get rid of him. In the 1850s he was put under police surveillance, his residence was monitored and his mail controlled. 'In the past few years, I've become *persona non grata*. I would have been exiled long ago as a revolutionary and the author of ungodly *Cosmos*, were it not for my position with the King. For the Pietists and the *Kreuzzeitung* crowd I am an abomination; they would be happy to see me six feet under.' His only protection was the king's support. The monarch treasured his chamberlain's presence because he was bored in Potsdam and turned a deaf ear to his courtiers' calumny of Humboldt.

What did Humboldt achieve with his strategy? When Frederick Wilhelm IV abolished slavery in his realm, the Minister of Justice wrote, 'The law promulgated owes its existence to Your Excellency's philanthropic intentions.' It was a modest and primarily symbolic victory as the abolitionists in England had pushed through a ban on slave trade half a century earlier. Other Humboldt initiatives were less obvious but far more consequential. He advocated for the rights of Jews and peasants. Humboldt also worked very successfully behind the scenes on science and education policy. Germany's prominence in science on the world stage in the second half of the nineteenth century is due, in no small part, to his example, his tenacious interventions and his skill in building an international network. You could even say that his silent diplomacy was aimed at aligning Germany with the West, a movement which became an irresistible force a century later.

All this had a cost. The inflexibility characteristic of revolutionaries like Georg Forster, Ludwig Börne or Karl Marx was not Humboldt's thing. He avoided attacking the existing political order head-on. The game he played with power was a complicated and contradictory one. Without cunning and mental reserves, he could not have managed it and this explains the ambiguity of his attitude. Humboldt lived a double life, not only erotically but also politically. He kept his cards very close to his chest and revealed his true intentions and convictions only to a few trusted friends. With much patience and irony, he suffered a great deal of boredom and vexation in the Potsdam court.

In old age, the shadow side of his brilliant life caught up with him. Perhaps every intellectual who tangles with power as Humboldt did must pay for his influence not only with any number of tactical compromises but also with a bottomless melancholy. Alexander von Humboldt was reproached for his vanity, perhaps justly. But was it a consolation for him to look back on a successful life? Hard to imagine. He was world famous but lonely. Here we have a final, existential paradox: the same man who authored countless communiqués and publications, who wrote nearly 50,000 letters and whose network spanned the world, ultimately found refuge in a place no one could follow him. In the last photograph of him, taken by Julius Siegmund Friedländer two years before Humboldt's death, he turns his eyes away from the viewer like an old Indian chief who harbours no more illusions about his own tribe or about politicians. This shot reveals a man who knew more than he said, who had his own thoughts on what was important to him, thoughts posterity will never be able to decipher.

MODELS OF NO VALUE

It has been a long time since I've heard anything from the National Family Forum and their project 'Children Need Values' and the side project 'Bringing Values to Life'. If I remember correctly, four clusters were formed along with the 'cluster-like planning group "The Religious Point of View".' The result of these efforts was the insight that the 'formation of competence in questions of values' is important. Since then not a peep. Why is that? Did the Federal Ministry for Family, Seniors, Women and Youth retract its generous support?

Naturally, in such cases, the private sector is sought out. The Commission on Values did not fail to do so. It stepped into the breach, proclaiming itself for 'six core values'. Among the 42 members of the advisory council is a certain *Herr* Hoppenstedt, a name that never fails to inspire whimsical ideas.

The commission's forum has no time for such amusement. They contacted 300 prominent figures and with a rather brusque demand: 'Your values, please!' Society's leaders did not hold back and shared their values freely. The chairman of the supervisory board of Roland Berger Strategy Consultants was able to declare with satisfaction that 'a return to values is indispensable'. The survey also led to the conclusion that 'lived values are playing an ever-greater role for leaders of German industry in guiding their companies and as a means of creating added value.' These values should not be considered only as a 'cyclic phenomenon but as a structural factor', since 'in times of upheaval, the influence of values as guiding principles increases.' More detailed information about the participants' individual values is available in a bound edition published by Gabler Verlag (192 pages, €39.95—order online from amazon.de!).

Even a well-financed apparatus like the Commission on Values would be overwhelmed with stuff and nonsense if it were ploughing a lonely furrow. Fortunately, that is not the case. The desperate search for values is supported by a dense network across the entire country of discussion groups, symposia, study groups, panel discussions and academies. These in turn all base themselves on an array of publications, of which I will name only a few: *The Origin of Virtues*; *The Book of Virtues*; *Values-Coaching in Times of Crisis*; *Is Germany Undergoing a Shift in Values?*, *Values in Times of Upheaval*; *Integrative Value Management*. These and many even more inane titles are available at any time. The ethics sector is booming.

One of the Commission's first tasks was to classify the flood of existing or imagined values in order to give a quasi-scientific appearance to their work. Yet, the swarm facing them is harder to tame than a sack of fleas. Nevertheless, these value ethicists were able to establish the following types of values: objective and subjective, external and internal, material and immaterial, individual and universal, spiritual, traditional, moral, aesthetic, ideal and religious. But look out! Each of these species has subspecies, as, for example, the Christian, Muslim, Buddhist, etc., along with their respective varieties, too numerous to list here.

You can hardly be blamed if this catalogue makes you dizzy. You will no doubt want to ask who is responsible for this woeful muddle. The explanation requires a brief detour into the history of philosophy. In any case, Immanuel Kant is not to blame. He had already made clear 200 years ago that talk of the 'absolute value' of good intentions is nothing more than a metaphorical plagiarism using the vocabulary of the economy. The executives concerned with the creation of added value know this too—the crux of the matter is, and remains, business and the only values that count in this sphere do not resemble those in the moral and intellectual spheres. These are monetary, exchange, net, fiduciary, book, market and currency values.

This routine confusion of types and genres can be traced back to a thinker who is widely forgotten today. His name is Hermann Lotze (1817–83). This professor from Göttingen is credited with being the founder of what is called 'the philosophy of values'. Indeed, he introduced these shady values into academic discourse and claimed that the 'feature of their reality' is simply their 'worth'. Other members of the philosophy faculty did not find this acceptable. Tedious debates ensued that cannot be summarized in a few words.

While a concept of *absolute value* saw values as defined by ideals independent of the human world, the concept of *ideal value* viewed them as ideal constructs like platonic ideas. The fundamental ontologist Nicolai Hartmann spoke of value's ideal *Ansichsein* [existing-in-itself]. This was not sufficient for Max Scheler, the founder of material value-ethics. He relied instead on his intuitive sense of value. The Neo-Kantians did not agree at all. They inclined to the view that values had their own realm in which they enjoyed unconditional worth but did not exist in a mode of being. Wilhelm Windelband countered this by raising the philosophy of value to a critical science of generally accepted values. He told anyone who asked that they formed the actual core of philosophy. Admittedly, for *moral relativists* values are simply correlates of a subjective value judgement.

This is all fine and dandy, if rather tedious. Yet it should not hide the fact that, on the philosophical stock exchange, share prices of the theories of value have fallen sharply. Perhaps this is because philosophers have never taken much interest in the values that make the headlines these days: levels of blood sugar, ozone, cholesterol, strontium or dioxin.

This does not mean we should drape the merciful cloak of oblivion over the philosophy of value. On the contrary! Its triumph is assured on any talk show addressing actual or fabricated crises. This is a vast field of action. The competition is fierce and the choice is difficult. Still, I should perhaps mention two particularly penetrating windbags and offer a taste of their talents. The American psychologist Shalom H. Schwartz was not afraid of drawing up his own Theory of Basic Human Values based on 10 types of values that exist throughout the world. His German colleague, the business ethicist Karl Homann formulated the following definition: 'Values have a fundamentally hypothetical character. Just as applying an empirical hypothesis to concrete phenomena is meant to explain these phenomena while at the same time testing the hypothesis, bringing values to the decision-making process will result in the solution to a concrete problem and will test the values used as well as their effectiveness.' Pardon me? Never mind, doesn't matter.

Earlier cultures preferred to come to an agreement on vices and virtues, laws and taboos. These old norms may seem anachronistic but they obeyed a clear code to which everyone could relate. In contrast, the flabby consistency of our 'values' is revolting. We were never so bereft of value as we are today. That said, they should in no case be recycled. Then they might be endlessly re-valued and the palaver would never end.

IS SEX NECESSARY, AND IF SO, HOW?

At first no publisher wanted to print the manuscript, not least because of the comical illustrations of hastily drawn men, women and dogs. James Thurber and E. B. White called the book that finally was published in 1929: *Is Sex Necessary?*

Their publisher's worries were unfounded. The public revelled not only in the text but also in Thurber's drawings and the book ended up on the bestseller lists. Only the experts who felt slighted by several passages ignored the book. The critics, moreover, raised various political objections, which we will examine.

All the same, the book's topicality is beyond debate. John Updike, who wrote a lovely foreword to the 2004 edition (the original edition had a number of introductions, prologues and forewords), noted, 'Seldom has a book with "sex" in the title had so little good to say for it.' He attributed this to the fact that Thurber had felt sleeping with his wife was like sleeping with the Statue of Liberty.

The authors felt that even then two factors in our civilization were enormously overemphasized: aviation and sex.

In the case of aviation, persons interested in the sport saw that the problem was to simplify it and make it seem safer . . . Even so, the plain fact remained that very few people were fitted for flying. With sex, the opposite was true. Everybody was fitted for it, but there was a lack of general interest. The problem in this case was to make sex seem more complex and dangerous. This task was taken up by sociologists, analysts, gynaecologists, psychologists and authors; they approached it with a good deal of scientific knowledge and an immense zeal. They joined forces and made the whole matter of sex complicated beyond the wildest dreams of our fathers. The country became flooded with books.

There is little to add to this analysis and it fits the situation in Germany as well, although there is one fact that makes it a bit more severe in our case. Ever since the word 'sexuality' has been shrunk into a kind of shorthand, it has lost its charm in our culture more than in other countries. Following the inane Anglicism, we now 'have' sex or fun the way we 'have' debts or stomach cramps. This has raised the level of difficulty in the matter of sex to a degree Thurber and White and their sources could not have anticipated. They were caught in a blinkered tradition that could hardly be called anything other than sexist and phallocratic. They kept to a simple binary code, as if there were only two sexes. At the time, mention of a third gender was limited to insinuation, and perhaps that is why the authors neglected it in their otherwise ground-breaking study.

Fortunately we have made significant progress since then. Our contemporaries now have a proliferation of sexes at their disposal. Along with hetero-, homo-, retro-, and metrosexuals, we also have the category of bisexuals its various subcategories, although it is unclear if the latter shouldn't more aptly be considered tri- or quadri-sexuals. On the other hand, it is not difficult to distinguish between transvestites and transsexuals.

The German sexologist Volkmar Sigusch has found some new variants. In his new book, *Neosexualitäten: Über den kulturellen Wandel von Liebe und Perversion* [Neo-Sexualities: On the Cultural Transformation of Love and Perversion], he analyses new and old manifestations of sexual activity from the Love Parade and zoophilia to Viagra and cybersex. He is also the one credited with coining the term 'cissexuality'. He wanted to express the idea that what is considered the normal alignment of one's mental and physical sexualities cannot be taken for granted and that if there are transsexuals there must also be cissexuals. But the competition never rests. Cisgender became established as a technical term denoting the opposite of transgender and replacing older terminology for non-transgender people, such as 'born female (or male)' or 'genetically male (or female)' or 'biological male' or 'biological female'. Cis people are not rare, we are told, but are quite common.

The enormous increase in the number of options that have surfaced since Thurber and White is undeniable. The good news is that the decision to define oneself as cis or trans or any other variant is a matter of negotiation, although questions arise in civil registry and passport offices as well as among health insurance adjusters in deciding which medical interventions and therapies should be covered. Another relatively new development is that all those concerned—and who isn't?—are encouraged, if not expected, to have an official *coming out*. This assumes among the less worldly a certain level of familiarity with English terms since there is no German word for it.

Otherwise the sexual enlightenment has spread across the board thanks to countless magazine articles, talk shows, advice columnists, advocacy and self-help groups. Our opening question whether sex is necessary is easily answered on the whole with a resounding yes.

One need worry only about the number of those who disagree. There are those who, for whatever reason, adhere to the strictest rules of chastity and cling to all manner of taboos. Some even respond to the previously unknown range of choices with overt hostility. Most are found among the heteronormative, and it can be assumed that they're prone to discriminating against others. Hence the critical tone that generally sticks to the term heteronormative. Sometimes they are even suspected of sympathizing with the Taliban, the mullahs or the Ultraorthodox, and quietly favouring stoning and caning.

Surely that goes too far. On the other hand, in a free society, tolerance and consideration must also be accorded those who have lost perspective over the increasing array of choices, who are displeased by the new enlighteners' zeal, or who simply want to be left in peace because they are as tired of the sexuality circus as Misters Thurber and White once were.

None of this is reason to get upset. The progress we have made is neither cause for cultural pessimism nor pride. A look at the rich heritage of earlier epochs will instil a degree of modesty. Compared with what we learn from ancient sources, contemporary neosexuality is decidedly colourless, if not staid. If our sexologists could be bothered to study them, they would turn green with envy.

They would find even in the holy scriptures the most dissolute fantasies, like the story of Sodom and Gomorrah or the sadomasochistic particulars of the Old Testament and the *Immerwährender Heiligenkalender* [The Perpetual Calendar of Saints]. They might be led to new pastures by the story of the Immaculate Conception, which should not be confused with the virgin birth.

These hair-raising revelations, however, seem all but harmless compared to the ancient Greeks' uninhibited indulgences. From them we learn the beautiful Helen hatched from an egg because Zeus impregnated her mother Leda disguised as a swan. Athena, the goddess of wisdom, sprang from her father's head in full armour after Hephaestus split his skull open with an axe. The father of the gods rained down on the Danae in a shower of golden rain. The son of Hermes and Aphrodite conjoined with a nymph so completely that their bodies melted into one body with male and female genitalia. There are other cases in which the protagonists themselves didn't know whether they were male or female. Pasiphaë, the King of Crete's wife, commissioned the obliging engineer Daedalus to build her a hollow cow because she has fallen in love with a bull. The bull was happy to be deceived and mounted the lady encased in the apparatus. The fruit of this rendezvous was a chimera, the Minotaur. Imaginative, but far from all that the ancient world has to offer. For lack of space, I will spare you the list of the pleasures, proclivities, castrations and rapes attributed to the Egyptians, Indians, Islanders and other peoples. Still, one hopes our sexologists will have the sense to admit that, compared to the authors of the *Mahabharata* and the *Metamorphoses*, they are babes in the woods.

OF COMMON SENSE AND ITS DEPRECATORS

Tossing around bits of English does not make for elegant German. Nevertheless, with regard to common sense, German speakers have no choice—we have no word for it. Our equivalent, *gesunder Menschenverstand* (sound judgement or healthy human reason), is not the same thing, since our *Menschenverstand* has often proved neither sound nor healthy. Older German citizens will remember how for 12 long years our reason was replaced by *gesunde Volksempfindung* [a Nazi neologism meaning 'sound public feeling'].

Let's just say that what is meant is the measure of natural intelligence inherent in most people or simply worldly wisdom, which we'd also like to believe is part of our natural inheritance. (Without a minimum of common sense, you're either foolish or insane.) Your average imaginary Englishman would no doubt also point to his practical sense, to his empiricism, to the way he solves everyday problems. 'By "a man of common sense" we mean one who knows, as we say, white from black, and chalk from cheese,' is the straightforward definition offered by Nicholas Amhurst, a forgotten eighteenth-century writer.

This simple statement should not disguise the fact that the organ we are dealing with is an extremely sensitive one. It is an instrument calibrated to detect immediately all that is pretentious, extravagant, convoluted. It is trained on lower things rather than the sublime. It is, therefore, represented in Greek mythology not by a goddess but by a servant who prefers to have her feet on the ground. Commonsensical thought would prefer risking platitudes to exaggeration.

Common sense behaves like the child in the Hans Christian Andersen fairy tale of the emperor's new clothes. It punctures all conceit and deflates all pompousness. To be sure, it is not out to garner attention like the troublesome child in the fairy tale. It pinches its lips and keeps its own counsel. It lacks the missionary zeal necessary for enlightening and improving others. It soon grows impatient but stubbornly sticks to its views. It reaches its most elevated form when sceptical of its own reason.

In the best case, common sense protects against dogmatic convictions lobbed by religious fanatics. It mistrusts the politicians' jargon and the louder the political propaganda, the harder it bounces off common sense's reservations. And yet it is no less fallible than other manifestations of the human spirit, most of whose more extravagant and luxurious materializations we would rather not renounce. It is a necessary but not sufficient talent. But like iron rations, it is indispensable to human reason. It is part of our subsistence minimum to which, *in extremis*, even the learned turn, hand on heart, although they may be loathe to admit it.

Common sense is often reproached with being narrow-minded, satisfied with banalities and not averse to frequenting the common folk, which is considered particularly objectionable. Most artists treat it with condescension. Their ultimate insult for it is *square*. Against genius, common sense doesn't stand a chance. Because where among the philistines does one find the excess, the originality, the break with comfortable habits and the ordinary way of seeing and hearing? In the world of art, the inveterate layperson only has a place as a patron or a member of the paying public, at least as long as he doesn't form an independent opinion.

But the commonsensical aren't any better tolerated by scientists. They will be considered ignorant since their objections are trivial. They can't begin to understand the bizarre logic of quantum theory. True, quantum theory can make experts dizzy, even if their calculations are correct. Common sense is also immune to the tenets of psychoanalysis, which its adepts can only ascribe to resistance and repression. The latest suggestions from neuroscience get no purchase either, when they want to persuade those full of common sense that they don't know what they're doing, only their brain does.

As fond as it is of ridiculing the theories experts try to frighten it with, common sense is still not hard to fool. It prefers estimation to calculation. Any mathematician can catch it out with trick questions. It cannot be dissuaded from the conviction that after landing a dozen times on red, the roulette ball will necessarily fall on black with the next spin. Nor is common sense a match for the tricks of probability, calculus and statistics. Deep in its heart it still believes that the sun rises and sets, although every child knows appearances deceive.

And what do philosophers think of common sense? Since the pre-Socratics, philosophers have been intrigued, fascinated, repelled and confused by it. According to Plato, when Thales of Miletus, founder of the Ionian school of natural philosophy, fell into a well while gazing at the stars, his clever and witty Thracian servant mocked his desire to learn what was in the heavens when he didn't know what was under his feet. Plato added that this joke will always fit those who live in philosophy. Since then any theoretician stumbling over daily life will run up against this famous anecdote.

It took a few sturdy philosophers of the Scottish Enlightenment to give the Thracian servant a measure of philosophical dignity. In the eighteenth century, Thomas Reid took on that task in *Inquiry into the Human Mind on the Principles of Common Sense*. The German Idealists expressed their indignation. Hegel was no more taken with Reid than Fichte or Schelling were.

Hegel writes:

This 'sound common sense' which takes itself to be a solid, realistic consciousness is [. . .]

always at its poorest when it fancies itself to be the richest. Bandied about by these vacuous 'essences', thrown into the arms first of one and then of the other, striving by its sophistry to hold fast and affirm alternately first one of the 'essences' and then the directly opposite one, it sets itself against the truth and holds the opinion that philosophy is concerned only with mental entities. As a matter of fact, philosophy does have to do with them too, recognizing them as the pure essences, the absolute elements and powers; but in doing so, recognizes them in *their specific determinateness* as well, and is therefore master over them, whereas perceptual understanding [or 'sound common sense'] takes them for the truth and is led on by them from one error to another.

Not everyone who reads this will be convinced.

Martin Heidegger reacted even more angrily to the servant's mockery, as would have been expected. For him the philosopher's accident, his loss of the ground beneath his feet and fall into the well, is precisely what should be admired. He considered philosophy, 'that thinking which, essentially, is of no practical use and about which housemaids necessarily laugh', to be on a far higher order than common sense.

Most readers will find the respect with which Ludwig Wittgenstein analysed word games in daily life more sympathetic, and they will find more comforting the attitude of Odo Marquard, who, furthermore, wrote with a graceful style—unlike George E. Moore, a renowned British philosopher who had such difficulties with ordinary language that he fell into the same well as Thales without a glance at the stars, putting the reader in the position of the Thracian servant. He had risen to the defence of common sense in a frequently quoted essay. Unfortunately, his attempt foundered on what his fellow philosophers call a *performative contradiction*.

This is a taste of Moore's argumentation:

> And I use the phrase, with regard to two facts, F1 and F2 . 'F1 is *logically dependent* on F2', wherever and only where F1 *entails* F2, [. . .] To say, then, of two facts, F1 and F2, that F1 is *not* logically dependent upon F2, is only to say that F1 *might* have been a fact, even if there had been no such fact as F2; or that the conjunctive proposition . . .

With such advocates, there's no need for detractors.

There is probably no need to be concerned for common sense. It is, like grass, hard to eradicate and it will easily survive not only its detractors but also its advocates.

COSMIC SECRET

If you never look at the ground, you might not notice the spots plastered all over the subway platforms and other subterranean surfaces. These trodden remains of chewing gum—of which 580,000 tonnes are consumed worldwide every year—are tenacious and hard to remove. It is easier to calculate the quantity of gum used than the benefit chewers expect from it.

When you see these sticky remains that disfigure our cities, do you also think of the 'services' that vaunt the fact that they are secret? Do you know that citizens in the United States shell out approximately 4 billion dollars each year for the pleasure of chewing gum? That is little compared to the 80 billion dollars budgeted for said services, not counting the additional 57 billion dollars allotted for the US Department of Homeland Security. One naturally wonders what the point of it all is. Gum is chewed not only in the United States but also across the world, which brings us back to our dirty pavements. Like chewing gum, the secret services also leave their traces all over the world.

Such comparisons can, of course, be taken too far. Are there, in fact, similarities between the secret services and chewing gum? I offer you four.

1. Squashed chewing gum tries to blend in. This discretion is characteristic of the intelligence services. Their collaborators prefer not to be listed in the telephone directory. They fob off the curious as best they can. Their headquarters take up a lot of space and often resemble fortresses but they also have at their disposal any number of fake addresses, secret apartments and safe houses, which our kind tends to overlook because the names under the doorbell like 'Jimmy Ballantine Pasteboard Ltd'

2. The secret services are as difficult to get rid of as blobs of chewing gum. No passer-by wants to get stuck with them, since he will have a hard time disentangling himself.

3. The sheer number of services is astounding. Apparently, like spots on the pavement, there can never be just one of them. In the United States, the official number of secret services is 17, with such attractive names as NSA, DIA, DHS, NRO, FBI, CIA, DEA, CNTOP, etc. Those services that are so secret, their existence must remain hidden are, of course, not mentioned. Russia, which is widely recognized as being ruled by the KGB, also has a broad range of secret services, including the GRU, SVR, FSB, FSO and the FAPSI. Countries like Iran and Syria refuse to trail behind such trendsetters. Acronyms also rain down upon the Federal Republic of Germany. Along

with the BKA, BND, MAD, BSI, IKTZ, FND and ZKA, each German state has its own LKA and its own LfV. In addition to these, we have the State Security sections in all police departments. In such a crowded field, it's no wonder toes get stepped on. It's also easy to get lost in the French labyrinth of Secretariat Generals, Directorate Generals, Central Directorates, Directorates and Brigades, all of whom eye each other jealously.

A commendable, albeit not exhaustive, collection in the Internet lists, if I counted correctly, 192 active 'services' from Afghanistan to Uzbekistan. A swarm of incomprehensible acronyms fill the entries, from ABIN to VEVAK and from ADIV to ÚZSI. Like a flag and a national anthem, these apparatuses seem to belong to the subsistence level of an independent state, even for countries that tend to be overlooked like Burundi or Malawi.

4. One last point of resemblance is the peculiarly tenacious consistency of the two entities. Nothing really affects the members of this guild. They are immune to changes in governments or regimes, lost wars—Cold and hot, ideological about-turns, and the collapse of empires. Cleaning them up would not be unlike sending an army of cleaners to remove dried chewing gum from ground. The German intelligence service, a successor to Wehrmacht General Reinhard Gehlen's organization, hired former Nazis and recruited unemployed SS and SA officers of all ranks. 'The German Federal Criminal Police Office

was even more egregious. At times, former members of the SS Death's Head Units held more than two thirds of all higher positions.' The personnel rosters of the post-Communist countries show a similar continuity. For their part, Western democracies have never shown much reluctance to deal with friendly dictators.

It goes without saying that the term 'service' is not to be understood literally. For as long as they've been around, these organizations have behaved like masters rather than public servants. Their leaders, from the president of the United States to monarchs and chancellors, all know that they themselves are under their henchmen's surveillance. They fear the dossiers compiled by the intelligence services, who, like J. Edgar Hoover, start from the premise that there is no one who cannot be blackmailed. This had been their precursors' premise as well: Joseph Fouqué in France as well as guards of the Okhrana in Tsarist Russia.

No secret service likes to be controlled. It prefers to operate in a moral, political, and legal grey area. In democratic states, such control is legally required. In Germany, the Bundestag established the BVerfSchG, BNDG, TBG, SÜG and the PKGrG. A parliamentary commission oversees questionable situations, but they meet in secret and do not report to any body.

Given the nature of the thing, a certain level of megalomania is not surprising. Because they have access to privileged information, members of the services consider themselves among the initiated. Their status symbol is the security clearance. On the one hand, there is an attempt to restrict classified knowledge to a minimal number of people. On the other hand, no less than 850,000 Americans have access to top-secret information. In NATO, the categories go from *Classified* to *Cosmic Top Secret*. This highest level is reserved for people who seem convinced that the entire universe has taken note of their existence.

Along with self-importance, paranoia is also part of the secret service's mental kit. It's perfectly normal that they smell enemy action, infiltrators, manipulators, moles and traitors everywhere. The 'meta-secret' is the most closely guarded of all, since it ensures that everything that should be kept secret will be. The secret services' acute self-reference is also striking. They expend a great deal of energy ferretting out moles and double agents in their own ranks. John Le Carré, a great connoisseur of the milieu, devoted entire novels to this shadow-boxing. The habitus of the secret services resembles the inner workings of sects in more than one respect.

This would be tolerable if the threat came only from their official enemies, but each clan believes itself embattled by colleagues from a competing apparatus. This means that each department keeps its information strictly to itself. It's regrettable that this behaviour borders on sabotage, however, since each organization protects its own interests, there is no way to avoid this.

Of course, external enemies who present an obvious danger are essential to the institution's survival. The more unbridled and brutal their adversaries, the better. Every successful assassination reinforces the secret services' indispensability. If there is a shortage of dangerous situations, they will take emergency measures, like sending in an *agent provocateur*, to ensure the conflict escalates. The methods of the Russian secret police under the Tsar as well as under Lenin and Stalin can serve as an example. Their Western counterparts have learnt many lessons from them. Compared to their expertise, the dilettantish provocations with which the German authorities tried to raise tensions in divided Berlin during the Cold War are modest indeed.

Why do the intelligence services fascinate the public so much, unlike other bureaucratic departments like the tax authorities? Why do so many believe that the agents' lives are filled with danger and adventure, and why do they observe the agents' activities with a mixture of trepidation and pleasure? We can thank the unflagging zeal with which the media revere them. Headlines, cover stories and countless films and novels feed on the spy legends they invent. And for that, we must acknowledge the secret services do have a certain level of usefulness, no matter that the crucial secret on which the world's survival depends is only ever hinted at. This doesn't reduce the fiction's entertainment value one bit. John Le Carré, the most sharp-witted author of the genre, knew very well why he called his troop's headquarters

the *Circus*. Even the parodies, in which James Bond caricatures the figure of the secret agent, have an undying public appeal.

These gullible consumers would no doubt be bitterly disappointed if they gained access to the heavily secured offices in which intelligence employees listen to radio broadcasts from North Korea and Tehran or translate bits of newspaper articles to put in files or databanks. In the Stasi's Berlin headquarters, everyone was able to witness the terrible boredom that reigns in such institutions. But those who operate outside the offices cannot generally expect a comfortable pension. In the ranks of these informants are no shortage of ruined lives, dubious quasi-criminal and psychologically devastated figures. Only a few silver coins from the services' well-stocked coffers fall to these helpers. In these circumstances, the word trust takes on a perverse meaning, as these agents must themselves be continuously watched, spied on, blackmailed if necessary, and occasionally sacrificed as fall guys.

A catalogue of fiascos, breakdowns, embarrassments and busts attributable to the secret services would fill volumes. From the Bay of Pigs invasion to the stationing of Soviet rockets in Cuba, from the arming of Islamists in Afghanistan to the false report of Saddam Hussein's weapons of mass destruction, the American intelligence services have not exactly covered themselves with glory. Indications of the attack on 11 September 2001 were ignored because the rival service didn't pass them on. There is no lack of German parallels, from their dealings with the Red Army Faction to attacks perpetrated by neo-Nazis. They grotesquely overestimated the economic potential of the GDR, slept through the collapse of the Soviet Union and didn't notice the Arab Spring until it was too late. And the abductions, secret prisons, torture and illegal killing that have nothing to do with spying, all go on the American intelligence services' account.

There is absolutely no doubt that secret services are in a position to inflict damage and lead dirty wars. However, it's not clear what exactly they're good for. They have been able to develop without restraint for three reasons. The first is political. Each president, each head of state, each chancellor effects a sort of moral division of labour. He is responsible only for the visible part of the executive branch's work. He doesn't need to know what the secret services are up to. So he can deny responsibility at any time. This advantage sometimes entails a disadvantage. As for the rest, what Lyndon B. Johnson said of J. Edgar Hoover applies: 'It's probably better to have him inside the tent pissing out than outside the tent pissing in.'

At least industrial espionage, if conducted even somewhat intelligently, speaks for their relevance in global competition.

But finally, and this is decisive factor, society will accept every scandal, all illegalities and all revelations as long as they believe the services are ensuring their security. The more fear, the greater the acceptance. As long as this is the case, questions of cost and benefit are never even asked. The services will keep proliferating and their legacy will keep sticking to the soles of our shoes. But should anyone ever crack the nut of their *cosmic secret*, they will probably find an empty shell.

A FEW SOURCES

Whenever possible, I have quoted and cited from existing English translations of the works Enzensberger refers to as well as, of course, the original English publications. Where translations are not available, I have translated the quotations directly from the German edition and cited the original sources. [Trans.]

Microeconomics

ENZENSBERGER, Hans Magnus. *Fatal Numbers: Why Count on Chance* (Karen Leeder trans.). New York: Upper West Side Philosophers, 2011.

ESPOSITO, Elena. *The Future of Futures: The Time of Money in Financing and Society* (Elena Esposito and Andrew K. Whitehead trans). Cheltenham: Edward Egar Publishing, 2011.

MANDELBROT, Benoit, and Richard L. Hudson. *The Misbehavior of Markets: A Fractal View of Financial Turbulence*. New York: Basic Books, 2004.

MANDEVILLE, Bernard. *The Fable of the Bees: Or Private Vices, Publick Benefits* [1714]. Oxford: Clarendon Press, 1924.

VOGL, Joseph. *Das Gespenst des Kapitals*. Zurich: Diaphanes, 2010. [English translation: Joseph Vogl, *The Specter of Capital* (Joachim Redner and Robert Savage trans). Stanford: Stanford University Press, 2015.]

On Insoluble Problems

BAK, Per. *How Nature Works: The Science of Self-Organized Criticality.* New York: Springer, 1996.

GEÖTSCHEL, Martin, and Mandred Padberg. 'Die optimierte Odyssee' [The Optimised Odyssey], *Spectrum der Wissenschaft* 4 (1999).

SINGH, Simon. *Fermat's Enigma: The Epic Quest to Solve the World's Greatest Mathematical Problem.* New York: Walker, 1997.

WIKIPEDIA CONTRIBUTORS. 'Erdbebenvorhersage' [Earthquake Prediction], *Wikipedia, The Free Encyclopedia.* Available at: https://de.wiki-pedia.org/wiki/Erdbebenvorhersage (last accessed on 2 December 2017).

How to Invent Nations at Your Desk

ANDERSON, Benedict. *Imagined Communities: Reflections on the Origin and Spread of Nationalism.* London: Verso, 1983.

GAUSS, Karl-Markus. *Im Wald der Metropolen* [In the Forest of Cities]. Vienna: Zsolnay Verlag, 2010.

HAARMANN, Haral. *Lexikon der untergegangenen Völker* [Lexicon of Vanished Peoples] Munich: C.H. Beck, 2005.

HERDER, Johann Gottfried. *Volkslieder. Nebst untermischten anderen* Stücken. Leipzig: Zweiter Theil, 1779. [English translation: Johann Gottfried Herder, *Song Loves the Masses: Herder on Music and Nationalism* (Philip V. Bohlman Trans.). Berkeley: University of California Press, 2017.]

———. *Briefe zu Beförderung der Humanität: Zehn Sammlungen* [Letters for the Advancement of Humanity: Ten Collections]. Riga: J.G.H. Erstdruck, 1793–97.

HOBSBAWM, Eric, and Terence Ranger. *The Invention of Tradition.* Cambridge: Cambridge University Press, 1983.

KAUSEN, Ernst. 'Kaukasische Sprachen' [Caucasian Languages]. Available at: https://goo.gl/-ygJVot (last accessed on 2 December 2017).

TACITUS. *Agricola and Germania* (Harold Mattingly trans.). London: Penguin Classics, 2010.

Retirement Plans

DESTATIS. 'Deaths, Life Expectancy and Mortality Statistics'. Wiesbaden: Statistisches Bundesamt [Federal Statistical Office]. Available at: https://-goo.gl/kXbtSu (last accessed on 2 December 2017).

SOZIALGESETZBUCH 6 [Social Code, Book 6] (1 January 1991). §68 and §255e. Available in German at: https://goo.gl/-tg5iEC (last accessed on 2 December 2017). Pension calculation formula is based on Clauses 68 and 255e of *Das deutsche Sozialgesetzbuch* [German Social Code].

Six Billion Experts

BUNDESAGENTUR FÜR ARBEIT [Federal Employment Agency]. *Schüsselverzeichnis für die Angaben zur Tätigkeit in den Meldungen zur Sozialversicherung* [Index for Declaration of Occupation in Registration for Social Insurance]. Federal Employment Agency: Nürnberg, 2010.

CHARISIUS, Hanno. 'Der unsichtbare Wald der Ozean' [The Ocean's Invisible Forest], *Frankfurter Allgemeine Sonntagszeitung* (21 August 2011).

FABRE, Jean-Henri. *The Insect World of J. Henri Fabre* (Alexander Teixeira de Mattos trans.). New York: Dodd, Mead and Co., 1949.

PLENDERLEITH, Harold J., and A. E. A. Werner. *The Conservation of Antiquities and Works of Art*. Oxford: Oxford University Press, 1971.

WIKIPEDIA CONTRIBUTORS. 'Artenvielfalt' [Biodiversity], *Wikipedia, The Free Encyclopedia*. Available at: https://-de.wikipedia.org/wiki/Artenvielfalt (last accessed on 2 December 2017).

The Pitfalls of Transparency

BENZ, Wolfgang. *Die Protokolle der Weisen von Zion. Die Legende von der jüdischen Weltverschwörung* [The Protocols of the Elders of Zion: Legends of Jewish World Conspiracy]. Munich: C. H. Beck, 2007.

JUNCKER, Jean-Claude. Quoted in 'Die Brüsseler Republik' [The Brussels Republic] by Dirk Koch, *Der Spiegel* 52 (27 December 1999). Available at: https://-/goo.gl/4FEioBl (last accessed 12 December 2017.)

STEINER, Rudolf. *An Outline of Occult Science* (Maud and Henry B. Monges trans). Dornach: Rudolf Steiner Press, 1972.

WEBER, Max. *The Political and Social Theory of Max Weber* (Wolfgang J. Mommsen ed.). Chicago: University of Chicago Press, 1989. Weber first mentions 'disenchantment of the world' in his 1917 lecture.

Poor Orwell!

BRADBURY, Ray. *Fahrenheit 451*. New York: Ballantine, 1953.

LA BOÉTIE, Étienne de. *The Politics of Obedience: The Discourse of Voluntary Servitude* (Harry Kurz trans.). New York: Columbia University Press, 1942.

ORWELL, George. *1984*. London: Secker and Warburg, 1949.

WEBER, Max. *The Political and Social Theory of Max Weber* (Wolfgang J. Mommsen ed.). Chicago: University of Chicago Press, 1989.

The Delightful Displeasures of Culture

BRETON, André. 'Second Surrealist Manifesto' in *Mani-festoes of Surrealism* (Richard Seaver and Helen Lane trans). Ann Arbor: University of Michigan Press, 1969.

DESTATIS. *Statistisches Jahrbuch für die Bundesrepublik Deutschland* [Annual Abstract of Statistics for the Federal Republic of Germany]. Wiesbaden: Statistisches Bundesamt [Federal Statistical Office], 2011. Available at: https://goo.gl/hw6bXD (last accessed on 2 December 2017).

DIE KÜNSTLERSOZIALKASSE [German Artists' Social Security Fund]. Official website. Available at: https://goo.gl/-DSJvFV (last accessed on 2 December 2017).

HANDKE, Peter. 'Offending the Audience' in *Handke Plays: 1* (Tom Kuhn trans.). London: Methuen, 1997.

HAAK, Carroll. *Wirtschaftliche and soziale Risiken auf den Arbeitsmärkten von Künstlern* [Economic and Social Risks for Artists in the Job Market]. Wiesbaden: VS Verlag, 2008.

MURGER, Henri. *The Bohemians of the Latin Quarter* (Ellen Marriage trans.). London: Greening and Co., 1901.

PUCCINI, Giacomo. *La Bohème: An Opera in Four Acts* (Premiered on 1 February). Turin: Teatro Regio, 1896.

ROSENKRANZ, Karl. *Ästhetik des Häßlichen*. Königsberg: Gebrüder Bornträger, 1853. [English translation: Karl Rosenkranz, *Aesthetics of Ugliness* (Andrei Pop and Mechtild Widrich trans). London: Bloomsbury, 2015.]

As If

BAUDRILLARD, Jean. *Simulacra and Simulation* (Sheila Glaser trans.). Ann Arbor: University of Michigan Press, 1994.

MERCK AND CO. 'Munchausen Syndrome' in *The Merck Manual of Diagnosis and Therapy*. Charleston: Nabu Press, 2011.

PLINY. *Natural History: A Selection* (John F. Healy trans.). London: Penguin, 1991.

VAIHINGER, Hans. *The Philosophy of 'As If': A System of the Theoretical, Practical and Religious Fictions of Mankind* (C. K. Ogden trans.). New York: Harcourt, Brace and Co., 1925.

Whither Photography?

BARTHES, Roland. *Camera Lucida: Reflections on Photography* (Richard Howard trans.). New York: Hill and Wang, 1981.

BENJAMIN, Walter. 'Kleine Geschichte der Photographie' in *Das Kunstwerk im Zeitalter seiner technischen Reproduzierbarkeit*. Frankfurt am Main: Suhrkamp, 1963. [English translation: Walter Benjamin, 'Small History of Photography' in *On Photography* (Esther Leslie trans.). London: Reaktion Books, 2015.]

BLOSSFELDT, Karl. *Art Forms in the Plant World*. New York: Erhard Weyhe, 1929.

DASTON, Lorraine, and Peter Galison. *Objectivity*. Brooklyn: Zone Books, 2007.

KING, David. *The Commissar Vanishes: The Falsification of Photographs and Art in Stalin's Russia*. New York: Metropolitan Books, 1997.

RENGER-PATZSCH, Albert. *Die Welt ist Schön* [The World is Beautiful]. Munich: Kurt Wolff Verlag, 1928.

SONTAG, Susan. *On Photography*. New York: Farrar Straus and Giroux, 1977.

Ordinary Miracles

HOBBES, Thomas. *Leviathan or The Matter, Forme and Power of a Common Wealth Ecclesiasticall and Civil* (Ian Shapiro ed.). New Haven: Yale University Press, 2010.

PRIGOGINE, Ilya. *Order out of Chaos*. New York: Bantam, 1984.

STEWART, Ian. *Does God Play Dice? The New Mathematics of Chaos*. Oxford: Blackwell, 1989.

VALÉRY, Paul. *Mauvaises Pensées et autres*. Paris: Gallimard, 1942.

Honourable and Less Honourable Professions

BÄCHTOLD-STÄUBLI, Hanns, and Eduard Hoffmann-Krayer. *Handwörterbuch des deutschen Aberglaubens* [Concise Dictionary of German Superstitions]. Berlin-Leipzig: Walter de Gruyter, 1927–42.

BENEKE, Otto. *Von unehrlichen Leuten* [On Dishonest People]. Berlin: Wilhelm Hertz, 1889.

MARX, Karl. 'Theories of Surplus Value' in Karl Marx and Friedrich Engels, *Collected Works*, VOL. 30. New York: International Publishers,1975.

MAYHEW, Henry. *London Labour and the London Poor* (Victor Neuburg ed.). London: Penguin,1985.

RADBRUCH, Gustav, and Heinrich Gwinner. *Geschichte des Verbrechens* [The History of Crime]. Stuttgart: K. F. Koehler, 1951.

Why Everything Always Leaves Spots

ENZENSBERGER, Christian. *Smut: An Anatomy of Dirt* (Sandra Morris trans.). London: Calder and Boyers, 1972.

DOUGLAS, Mary. *Purity and Danger: An Analysis of Concepts of Pollution and Taboo*. London: Routledge, 1966.

GIEDION, Sigfried. *Mechanization Takes Command: A Contribution to Anonymous History*. New York: Oxford University Press, 1948.

HOMER. *The Odyssey* (A. T. Murray trans.). Cambridge, MA: Harvard University Press. Book IV, lines 85–95, 1919.

LICHTENBERG, Georg Christoph. *Sudelbücher* (Wolfgang Promies ed.). Munich: Hanser Verlag, 1968. [English translation: Georg Christoph Lichtenberg, *Lichtenberg: Aphorisms and Letters* (Franz H. Mautner and Henry Hatfield eds and trans). London: Jonathan Cape, 1969.]

LUHMANN, Niklas. 'Systemtheoretische Argumentationen' [Systems Theory Argumentation] in *Theorie der Gesellschaft oder Sozialtechnologie* [Theory of Society or Social Technology] (Jürgen Habermas and Niklas Luhmann eds). Frankfurt: Suhrkamp, 1971.

SMULDERS, Eduard. *Laundry Detergents*. Weinheim: Wiley-WCH, 2002.

It's a Gift!

BATAILLE, Georges. 'The Notion of Expenditure' in *Visions of Excess: Selected Writings, 1927–1939* (Allan Stoekl trans.). Minneapolis: University of Minnesota Press, 1985.

CLASTRES, Pierre. *Society Against the State: Essays in Political Anthropology* (Robert Hurley trans.). Brooklyn: Zone Books, 1987.

MALINOWSKI, Bronislaw. *Argonauts of the Western Pacific*. London: Routledge, 1922.

MAUSS, Marcel. *The Gift: Them and Reason for Exchange in Ancient Societies* (W. D. Halls trans.). New York: Norton, 1990.

SLOTERDIJK, Peter. 'The Grasping Hand: The Modern Democratic State Pillages its Productive Citizens' (Alexis

Cornel trans.), *City Journal* (Winter 2010). Available at: https://goo.gl/SrrLfb (last accessed on 2 December 2017).

Is Science a Secular Religion?

EINSTEIN, Albert. Letter to Eric Gutkind (3 January 1954). Available at: https://goo.gl/eHC6hp (last accessed on 2 December 2017).

FEYERABEND, Paul. *Against Method: Outline of an Anarchist Theory of Knowledge*. New York: New Left Books, 1975.

HÜBNER, Kurt. *Critique of Scientific Reason* (Paul R. Dixon trans.). Chicago: University of Chicago Press, 1983.

HÜLSWITT, Tobias. 'Im Gespräch: Werden wir ewig leben, Mister Kurzweil?', *Frankfurter Allgemeine Sonntagszeitung* (13 February 2008).

KUHN, Thomas. *The Structure of Scientific Revolutions*. Chicago: University of Chicago Press, 1962.

LA METTRIE, Julien Offray de.*Man a Machine* (Richard A. Watson and Maya Rybalka trans). Indianapolis: Hackett, 1994.

POLANYI, Michael. *The Tacit Dimension*. New York: Doubleday, 1967.

———. *Meaning*. Chicago: University of Chicago Press, 1975.

Alexander von Humboldt and the Battle Between Intelligence and Power

BOTTING, Douglas. *Humboldt and the Cosmos*. New York: Harper and Row, 1973.

ETTE, Ottmar. *Alexander von Humboldt und die Globalisierung*. Frankfurt am Main: Insel Verlag, 2009.

HUMBOLDT, Alexander von. *Letters of Alexander von Humboldt to Varnhagen von Ense. From 1827 to 1858* (Friedrich Kapp trans.). London: Rudd and Carleton,1860.

————. *Gespräche Alexander von Humboldts* [Alexander von Humboldt's Conversations] (Hanno Beck ed.). Berlin: Akademie Verlag, 1959.

KRÄZ, Otto. *Alexander von Humboldt: Wissen-schaftler, Welt-bürger, Revolutionär* [Alexander von Humboldt: Scientist, World Citizen, Revolutionary]. Munich: Callwey, 1997.

Models of No Value

BUNDES FORUM KINDER- UND JUGENDREISEN [National Forum for Child and Youth Travel]. Official website. Available at: www.bundesforum.de (last accessed on 2 December 2017).

KANT, Immanuel. *Groundwork of the Metaphysic of Morals* (H. J. Paton trans.). New York: Harper Torchbooks, 1956.

LOTZE, Hermann. *System of Philosophy* (Bernard Bosanquet trans.). Oxford: Clarendon Press, 1884.

WERTEKOMMISSION. Official website. Available at: https://goo.gl/Q6VSVH (last accessed on 2 December 2017).

WIKIPEDIA CONTRIBUTORS. 'Wertvorstellung' [Value Proposition], *Wikipedia, The Free Encyclopedia*. Available at: https://de.wikipedia.org/wiki/Wertvor-stellung (last accessed on 2 December 2017).

————. 'Axiologie' [Axiology], *Wikipedia, The Free Encyclopedia*. Available at: https://de.wikipedia.org-/wiki/Axiologie_(Philosophie) (last accessed on 2 December 2017).

WINDELBAND, Wilhelm. *History of Philosophy*, 2nd EDN (James H. Tufts ed. and trans.). New York: Mac-millan, 1901.

Is Sex Necessary, and If So, How?

OVID. *Metamorphoses* (Charles Martin trans.). New York: Norton, 2005.

SELLNER, Albert Christian. *Immerwährender Heiligen-kalender* [The Perpetual Calendar of Saints]. Frankfurt: Eichborn Verlag, 1998.

SIGURSCH, Volkmar. *Neosexualitäten. Über den kulturellen Wandel von Liebe und Perversion* [Neosexualities: On the Cultural Transformation of Love and Perversion]. Frankfurt: Campus Verlag, 2005.

SMITH, John D. (ed. and trans.). *The Mahabharata*. London: Penguin, 2009.

THURBER, James, and E. B. White. *Is Sex Necessary? Or Why you Feel the Way You Do*. New York: Harper and Brothers, 1929.

WIKIPEDIA CONTRIBUTORS. 'Cisgender', *Wikipedia, The Free Encyclopedia*. Available at: https://en.wikipedia.org/-wiki/Cisgender (last accessed on 2 December 2017).

———. 'Transgender', *Wikipedia, The Free Encyclopedia*. Available at: https://en.wikipedia.org/wiki/Transgender (last accessed on 2 December 2017).

Of Common Sense and Its Deprecators

AHURST, Nicholas. *Terrae-filius, Or The Secret History of the University of Oxford (1721)*. Newark: University of Delaware Press, 2004.

HEGEL, G.W.F. *Phenomenology of Spirit* (A.V. Miller trans.). Oxford: Oxford University Press, 1977.

HEIDEGGER, Martin. *What is a Thing?* (W.B. Barton and Vera Deutsch trans). Washington DC: Gateway Editions, 1970.

MOORE, G. E. *Philosophical Papers*. New York: Collier Books, 1962.

PLATO. *Theaetetus* [Dialogues of Plato] (Benjamin Jowett trans.). Oxford: Clarendon, 1892.

REID, Thomas. *An Inquiry into the Human Mind on the Principles of Common Sense*. London: T. Cadell, 1764.

SCHMIDT, Alfred. 'Sind Philosophen Verrückt?: oder Wittgenstein und das Lachen der thrakischen Magd', *Biblos* (2001). Available at: https://goo.gl/-4a5Xk4 (last accessed on 2 December 2017).

Cosmic Secret

BAKER, Russell. Lyndon B. Johnson quoted in 'Overgrown Boys', *New York Review of Books* (12 January 2012).

BESTE, Von Ralf, Georg Bönisch, Thomas Darnstädt, et al. 'Welle der Wahrheiten' [Wave of Truth], *Der Spiegel* 1 (2012). Available at: https://goo.gl/-kdkNQM (last accessed on 2 December 2017).

GEHEIMDIENSTE [Secret Services]. Information Portal on Intelligence Services and Intelligence Services. Available at: https://goo.gl/PGz1rd (last accessed on 2 December 2017).

LAPORTE, Maurice. *Histoire de l'Okhrana: La Police secrète des tsars, 1880–1917* [History of the Okhrana: The Secret Police of Tsars]. Paris: Payot, 1935.

PRIEST, Dana, and William M. Arkin. *Top Secret America: The Rise of the New American Security State*. New York: Little, Brown and Co., 2011.

WIKIPEDIA CONTRIBUTORS. 'Liste der Nachrichtendienste' [List of News Services], *Wikipedia, The Free Encyclopedia*.

Available at: https://de.wikipedia.org/wiki/Liste_der_
Nachrichtendienste (last accessed on 2 December 2017).

————. 'Staatsschutz' [State Protection], *Wikipedia, The Free Encyclopedia*. Available at: https://de.wikipedia.org/-
wiki/Staatsschutz (last accessed on 2 December 2017).